PRAISE FOR

"What compels a young woman to enter the emotional minefield that is professional Christian ministry and keep working, despite despair that robs her of personal faith in God? With characteristic grace, brutal honesty, and detailed personal reflection, Marjorie Weiss describes what it was like to be leading congregations, encountering chronic loneliness, and dealing with systemic sexism while struggling with the mental and physical illnesses that engulfed her family for decades. It's a wonder she gets to the other side. Congratulations to Pastor Weiss for telling the truth about what private life can be like for women who seek to publicly serve the Church."

—Lynne Silva-Breen, MDiv, MA, LMFT, *Marriage and Family Therapist and former ELCA Pastor, Burnsville, Minnesota*

"A very human illustration of one seeking an authentic faith relationship with God, not just in joy but in struggle and heartache as well. Lutherans love to talk about the 'real presence' of Christ in ways that we can see and taste and touch. Pastor Weiss takes us on a journey that chronicles working through the 'real absence' of Christ, at times in her life. Seminarians, clergy and anyone who daily searches for a genuine faith relationship will find benefit from this work."

—Bruce G. Trethaway, MDiv

"Pastor Marjorie Weiss's history reveals that she is a risk-taker: one of the first female Lutheran pastors, an adoptive parent of an older child, a champion of her marginalized colleagues, and now an author divulging her innermost thoughts, fears and triumphs before the world. This honest and exposing memoir shows us a pastor who, in the depths of isolation, loneliness and pain, wonders if God does not exist. I wholeheartedly recommend this compelling journey of faith through the written word."

—Rev. John Hagedorn, PhD

"Upsetting, passionate, and lyrical seem like strange bedfellows, but in Marjorie Weiss's memoir they are natural companions. And let's not forget brave, for she has opened up areas of pain and revelation long buried in most human beings. This writer should be welcomed into the fold."

—Julie Gilbert, *Author and Pulitzer Prize-nominated Biographer*

PRAYING ON EMPTY

A Female Pastor's Story

To the uniquely
spelled Kathlene

Marjorie Weiss

PRAYING ON EMPTY

A Female Pastor's Story

MARJORIE WEISS

Photo by Mitch Kloorfain • Cover Design by Rolf Busch

Library of Congress Cataloging-in-Publication Data

Weiss, Marjorie

Praying on Empty: A Female Pastor's Story

p. cm.

Paperback ISBN: 978-1-947708-54-9

Ebook ISBN: 978-1-947708-56-3

Library of Congress Control Number: 2019932436

First Edition, June 2019

Murphy, North Carolina, USA

(828) 585 - 7030

www.CitrinePublishing.com

For Davey

I always knew.

Contents

PROLOGUE

June 2011

The day the idea entered my head to become a pastor should be cursed. That day might also be blessed. Such was the hate-love relationship that had developed regarding my ministry, my job, and my personal life. Did male clergy feel this way? I often wondered if the ping-pong ambivalence I felt regarding living and working as a pastor was unique to my female psyche or if it was gender-neutral. I trudged through the dunes of parish ministry, hoping that over the next rise there would be an oasis where God would be waiting to explain why this job was so *damned* hard. Yes, I swear and cuss. And I am not the only pastor who does, despite the reality that many think the clergyperson's mind zings with burning judgment whenever they hear someone swear. I like doing it. It's a cathartic action for my brewing volcano of issues.

Some oases—islands of refreshment—have existed throughout my years as a professional Christian: lives have been changed, the poor helped, and there are many people who have loved and supported me. Nevertheless, the God oasis was the one I NEEDED. There, God will greet me with a gin and tonic. Whether God is a man or a woman, I have not yet decided. I will sit down in the Adirondack chair offered, plant my feet in the sand, sip my favorite drink, with lime of course, and in true *I Love Lucy* style I will say, "God, you have some splainin' to do!" God will oblige with a chuckle and will make it clear that the personal sacrifices, the isolation, the loneliness, and the toleration (of people who have treated me in a most detestable manner) have all been worthwhile. I will require a great deal of convincing. Yet, our dialogue will give me hope.

I began these reflections a year ago in the month that I marked the thirty-year anniversary of my June 1, 1980, ordination into the Christian ministry. The 400-member Lutheran congregation, for which I served as pastor, had a party for the occasion, at which the genuine affection they had for me was most evident. The elegantly set tables and scrapbook (with individual pages of memories made by members) contrasted with their gentle "roast" of me, in which they poked fun at my years-long affection for *Star Trek* and the soap opera *Days of Our Lives.*

It was also the month in which I experienced an emotional breakdown, manifested in uncontrollable tears of gut-wrenching intensity. The sobbing lasted in some form for weeks and frightened me into an epiphany that screamed, "You have to learn how to live life differently or you will, at worst, not survive. At best, you'll live the rest of your employed years, or even of your life, in proverbial 'quiet desperation.' " My feelings continuously bounced like a ball, pinging and then ponging between love and hate. Such were my days when I wondered how I could be so good at what I did for a living and yet, was getting increasingly less satisfaction from it.

Additionally, that party was ten months since the day I had quite unexpectedly lost most, if not all, of my belief in God, at least the God I thought I had known. I found that I had become a pilgrim seeking a faith that had once been my touchstone, and was hoping for its resurrection. Simultaneously, I was considering the unsettling notion that my life would be most improved without God and without Christians surrounding me all the time. How had I gotten to this Sahara?

The Cinder Block Room

August 2009

The setting was beautiful: the Marriott Hotel which overlooked Biscayne Bay in Miami, Florida. My husband, David, and I were dining in the grand high-ceilinged restaurant, looking out at the sparkling water, the boats, and the happy bicyclists. Even though it was August and the summer's usual 90 degrees, the breezes from the nearby Atlantic had made our earlier walk pleasant despite the humidity. In a few days, we were to mark twenty-eight years of marriage. That evening, we looked upon the meal as our anniversary celebration, knowing that David would not be in any shape to go out to eat on our actual anniversary date. We were seventy miles from our home in order for him to undergo his second deep brain stimulation surgery (DBS) early the next morning.

Deep brain stimulation was still a relatively new treatment for the symptoms of Parkinson's disease (PD), which David had been diagnosed with (as young-onset) when he was fifty. "No problem," his doctor had initially said, "we can give you twenty more good years." This prediction was not to be. Unfortunately, Dave was one of the rare people who did not get relief from medication for the "Parkinsonianisms," which, for him, were tremors in his arms and legs, stiffness, rigidity, and daily suffering from pain in those extremities. His most recent neurologist at the time had tried every standard medication and then some. He had even prescribed him the highest dosage of Carbidopa/Levodopa (the medication of last resort) that any patient of his had ever used. The side effects of that high dose were extreme, but still his tremors continued unabated and were so debilitating that he could no longer lift a drink with one hand. He had had to revert to the two-handed child's way of cupping a glass. He was also having more and more difficulty getting a loaded fork to his mouth while eating. I had to carry his plate for him if we were at a buffet, which showed how he was increasingly dependent on me as a caregiver. His meds were eventually reduced since the high dose was clearly not effective. Consequently, the side effects that had put him on edge and ready to jump out of his skin had lessened, but his life became one of daily agony from the never-ending pain and frustration. His only relief was sleep because then he did not shake.

Depression is also a symptom of PD. For Dave, this meant additional depression on top of the clinical depression from which he had already been suffering for at least a dozen years before Parkinson's entered our lives. "What a joke this is," he said with dark humor. "Give a guy with depression a disease that makes a person depressed." That wasn't funny to me. Depression is often more hellish for the loved ones than the depressed person, and I had already noticed him diving ever deeper into the darkness. Such tumbles always pulled me under as well. At age fifty-five, his days were often ones of watching himself shake.

Illness is never experienced in isolation. Dave's combined pain from PD and depression became mine. It moved us into one of the most despairing times of our lives. At work I was often in a daze, trying to concentrate on my next sermon or on the person sitting across from me for counseling. I wrestled with hopelessness and then I would come home to this dark soul sitting on a chair, trying to read a book that often shook too much for him to follow a sentence. I prayed for Dave to die so that he would not be in such misery and, to be frank, so that I would not have to watch it. I envisioned him purposely driving himself into one of the Florida canals near our home to drown himself, and would have totally understood his motivation had he chosen to do so. I was helpless and tired of being his cheerleader since there was no chance of winning the game. Our future looked bleak. Parkinson's and depression were thieves, taking so much from us.

I never blamed God, nor did he. Getting Parkinson's is just bad luck. I totally reject any theology that casts God as a punisher, zapping people with pestilence in order to discipline them. I don't even understand Christians who can say "God is love" or "God is a loving father" and then try to come up with a reason for why God sent a bad thing into their lives. Do they not see the disconnection? Sometimes, as the bumper sticker proclaims, "Shit Happens." And it happened to him—to us.

Dave's daily life had become quite diminished and there was little for him to do since he was unable to utilize the small motor skills required to engage in his hobbies of camera repair and building radio-controlled cars. He was receiving disability income due to his inability to work in his profession of computer programming. A computer mouse does not cooperate with a tremoring hand. At the time, I thought he'd be in a nursing home before he was sixty.

However, salvation came in the form of DBS, a surgery in which an electro-stimulator is implanted into the portion of the brain affected by the disease. By sending high-frequency electrical impulses into that specific area, it can mitigate symptoms. Dave's first DBS surgery had been in October 2007 when a stimulator was implanted in the left side of his brain to control the tremors and stiffness on the right side of his body. Patients have to be semi-conscious—that means awake!—during the first part of the surgery in order to speak to the medical team to give them feedback regarding improvement. "Has your hand stopped shaking? How about now? Is your leg less stiff?" When the computer, doctors, and patient agree that the symptoms are mitigated, the patient is then put under general anesthesia so that electronic wires can be snaked under the skin from the skull, down the neck, to a battery implanted in the patient's chest or belly. I took David home the next day, amazed that brain surgery was just an overnighter. Three weeks post surgery, after he had healed during the recommend interval of time, the stimulator was turned on and Dave was wondrously given back much of his life. So was I.

His tremoring right hand, leg, and foot were still. The pulsing that I had always felt in his hand, when I held it during our walks, was quiet. Without a doubt, the best benefit was that he was pain-free, and the pinched visage that had become standard was relaxed and peaceful. Consequently, Dave's spirits improved and he even found that he could manage some of his hobbies. The PD continued to progress, but with the doctor making periodic computer adjustments of the electro-stimulator during office visits, he'd been given years of quality life that never would have been his otherwise.

Not quite two years later, similar PD symptoms had begun to affect his left side, resulting in tremors in his hand and leg and great pain in his arm and shoulder. He opted for a second DBS surgery on the right side of his brain. Hence, we were in Miami for our early anniversary dinner at the Marriott.

"I don't look forward to this, Margie, especially when they drill those holes into my skull to attach the metal halo. Man, did that ever hurt!"

I smiled sympathetically. "Well, I think you do want your head to stay still during the operation. You don't want an accidental lobotomy. I might like that but you, not so much." He stuck his tongue out at me.

The halo had hurt, but he had found the rest of the previous surgical procedure tolerable, and was even able to joke with the doctors during the "awake" portion of that surgery. He was confident that this next one would go smoothly. The benefits were going to be extraordinary, just as they had been from surgery number one. I thanked God for the technology that was keeping my husband from becoming a drooling, shuffling shadow of himself. I had seen that happen to my Uncle Howard, who had also had the disease. It was a terrible thing to watch.

For us, anniversaries are always a time to reminisce about our past, so we easily steered our conversation to what we had considered highlights of our years together. "You know when I knew I could love you?" he asked as his green eyes crinkled and disappeared into his deep-set sockets when he smiled at me with anticipation.

"Was it the tube top I was wearing when I invited you over for dinner?"

"No, but it was a surprise to see you for the first time in many years, a pastor no less, opening the door wearing that and short shorts."

"It was August and hot outside."

"I didn't mind it, you know."

"Just like I didn't mind the flowers and you standing there wearing a shirt and tie, your red hair shining. And you had the Vandyke beard I've always liked. You looked good—yummy."

"Ah, those were the days before I went bald."

I looked at his shining head and tried to remember him

with hair. "You look okay to me... Now, tell me when you thought you could love me."

"The next week after we went out for dinner, back at your apartment you tried to get me coffee and..."

"Dropped that bottle of Tabasco sauce on my dress."

"Yeah, it shattered on the counter. I was waiting in the living room, heard the crash and then you yelled, 'Shit!' Any pastor who said 'shit' was okay by me, especially a beautiful one!"

"I sure didn't feel beautiful in those days, with my odd and missing teeth, but you didn't seem to mind. It didn't take us long to fall for each other, did it?" I said with a smile revealing my now-beautiful teeth.

"Nope," Dave agreed, beaming. "And I never really noticed your teeth as a distraction, not like you did. But anyway, who would have thought that two people who were from the same hometown would have hooked up years later and have it click?" It certainly had been a marvel to us both and assisted in our bonding since we had common childhoods, teachers, and memories of our shared hometown of Oley.

Dessert came as the sun was setting on the bay and we moved into reflecting on our wedding and then our years together—the challenges and joys of raising our two daughters and how content we now were in the empty nest. We reviewed the three moves we had made to different communities for my church work, our vacations, the cats we had loved, and our big transition from Pennsylvania to Florida five years earlier. Dave's decade-long battle with depression had been won about a year before so it was fabulously pleasant to be enjoying each other's company with a lightness of energy around us.

Dave interrupted our reverie with an unexpected question. "Would you have married me if you knew I would get Parkinson's disease?"

I tried not to choke on my food. "What a question!" I laughed. But I could see by his expression that he actually wanted a serious answer. My response came surprisingly quickly.

"Parkinson's yes. Depression, no." His eyes grew large. "Those years of struggling with your depression were miserable for me and detrimental to our marriage."

"Yeah, but worse than Parkinson's?"

"Parky," I said (my nickname for his illness), "is manageable and predictable. We can plan for the inevitable. Mr. D," I continued (my nickname for his clinical depression), "was a specter living in our home—in you. I hated him. You know that. He was unpredictable, mean-spirited, and created a vacuum whenever he showed up, which was far too often. Mr. D was making you a dark shadow. He was a thief who took you from me. Compared to Mr. D, Parky is a walk in the park."

My husband's eyes shone at my play on words. "Parky, walk in the park—cute!" Then in sincerity said, "I didn't really know how much my depression affected you, you know that—"

"Since you were depressed," I interrupted and smiled back. "You always retreated into yourself when Mr. D showed up. It was infuriating...and lonely."

"But your saying it was worse than PD sure puts it into

perspective…I'm sorry." His eyes got misty and tears poured over. "I'm sorry for the way I was."

I grabbed his hand. "I know you are, but with Parky, I can't blame you. With depression it was so easy to hate you for what 'you' were doing to us and the family—to me—because it was hard to distinguish between illness and David. I lost you for so long. That happy man I married was stomped down by that damn brain chemistry fuck-up that caused your depression. Had I known in advance about how often I would wish you dead…" I began to tear over as well. "Because you left me while still existing in our home as that alien…No, I would not have walked down the aisle that day."

Clinical depression affects millions of people. One of God's blessings has been the development of antidepressants. Mr. D had been with us for years, maybe for most of our marriage in some form, without our knowing what he was. But as the years passed, he showed up more often and stayed longer as our lives became fuller with kids and our respective job demands. In 1997, sixteen years into our marriage, long before Parky showed up, Mr. D was diagnosed and revealed. Dave started using Prozac. The effect was stunning. Mr. D, the hostage-taker, let go for the majority of the time. My lacking-in-affect husband began to smile, laugh, and become more engaged with life. Work hassles no longer immobilized him. Alas, Prozac began to lose its effectiveness after a year or so, even with increases in dosage. His primary care physician, therefore, referred him to a psychiatrist.

Unlike actor and Scientology Golden Boy Tom Cruise, who famously ranted against psychiatry (as all Scientologists do) to Matt Lauer on *The Today Show*, I am glad for it. (I was so ticked off at Mr. Cruise that I have not seen a movie of his since that tirade as I assume he kept many depressed people from the help they could receive. I'm sure my boycott has cost this multi-millionaire at least $100.) Unfortunately, we had a lot of difficulties finding a psychiatrist who would treat Dave for more than what seemed to be ten minutes before his or her moving on to a new job in a new locale. As a result, he never had a medical professional who considered his entire health history. The medical center that served our HMO even had rent-a-docs, psychiatrists who were hired short-term for six months to fill in holes in the staffing schedule. Dave saw a stream of these temps who gave him pills and nothing more. If only one of them would have probed to see if the medication and dose were really helping him. His sessions were done in fifteen minutes. Shockingly, no such thing as psychotherapy ever happened. His condition never improved. In fact, it often declined. Suicide watch was at times mine.

Mr. D grew stronger while David grew weaker, caught in their battle for prominence. I was miserable living with Dave's negativity and disinterest in life. Our daughters were mercifully indifferent as kids can be regarding parental trials. In 2004, seven years after he began antidepressants, we moved to Florida for my job. That stressful transition caused his depression and anxiety to lurk vulture-like, waiting to devour what was left of "us." He was already two years into the travails of PD at that time, so Parky and Mr. D worked in tandem. Divorce was not a reality that I considered, nor did he, although I fantasized about the "freedom" it might give me from Mr. D. However, when Mr. D was at bay, Dave was an excellent life partner and great support for me in my work. I loved him.

We were both pleased when, after failing with two psychiatrists in our new state—both pill-oriented and nothing more—Dave found a new psychiatrist, Dr. Hunter. She was the first one who spent time with him, interviewing him during each appointment to determine what medication would be best. She asked him about his mood, his life, and his thought patterns. This was new and wonderful. She even found a medication that simultaneously treated his depression and helped him get some relief from the leg pain in the months before his first DBS. I considered her a blessing and a lifeline from God. I always sat in on his appointments since I was now the driver for long trips. Dave could no longer handle driving very far because his foot shook too much. I also had to be his short-term memory, since PD took some of that ability from him. Dr. Hunter truly wanted to help my husband get better. She gave us hope.

On our fourth appointment, we walked into her office and she immediately began to berate him. "Mr. Derr, when you started at my practice you filled out paperwork that asked you if you were attempting to get disability coverage. You said no, but here I am with all this paperwork sent to me about your filing for disability with the government." (After we had moved to Florida Dave could no longer work so we were glad for a personal disability policy he had that supplemented his lost income. At the time of this incident, we had just filed for Social Security disability benefits as well.)

Dave's bewilderment matched mine when he asked, "What's the issue, doctor? I don't understand."

"No, of course, you act like you don't understand. You're just trying to get disability. I took you on in good faith and now you're costing me hundreds of dollars in paperwork and time."

Dave tried to explain. "It's true that I wasn't pursuing disability coverage when I began here. I didn't lie. We began the process based on my Parkinson's, later, not because of my depression and anxiety. We sure could use the money since I can't work anymore."

She cut him off and continued to disparage him and then me, essentially calling us unethical and telling us we would have to pay her $750 to fill out the paperwork. She also intimated that she would no longer treat him. I tried to understand what was happening and why she was so angry. As her rant droned to mush in my hearing, I saw my dream of her healing my husband begin to dematerialize. Humiliation rose in me when I could not control my tears. Interrupting the doctor, I turned to Dave and tried to talk, which was difficult as I was near full-out bawling. "Dave, I'm going out to the car...I can't stay here. . . I'll wait for you there."

I darted down the hall past the receptionist and out the door, trying to breathe and not fall into a heap. But crumple is what I did when I got out to the parking lot. I sat on a curb in the hot sun and sobbed uncontrollably for I don't know how long. A half hour? More, maybe. Every time I tried to stop, I couldn't. Thoughts raced through my mind. *What the hell is wrong with me? Why isn't Dave coming out? How could Dr. Hunter have been so dreadful? I'm all alone. There is no one who understands what I go through.* And finally, "God, help me!" I implored aloud. I believed that God was listening and would give me strength.

Dave eventually came out to tell me that he and Dr. Hunter had come to an understanding and she finally had acknowledged that we weren't like patients who saw her just to try to get disability. She was sorry for her words and sorry she had made me cry. Too late, the damage was done. The feelings of trauma and betrayal from Dr. Hunter blindsiding us in that way have stayed with me. When I speak of it now, I can return to those feelings and the isolation I felt in that moment. I had lost my only advocate in my battle with Mr. D because I could no longer trust her.

Amazingly, two years later, after we had gladly left Dr. Hunter's practice, Mr. D finally ran for the hills when Dave began a regimen of fish oil and cod liver oil daily. I'd read about their benefits for depression and that was the cure for him. His brain needed the omega-3 fatty acids, is our guess. Something so simple essentially banished a depression that had been with him for a decade. He no longer uses any medication for depression or anxiety. Mr. D still tries to visit. Anxiety is a companion, but when Dave becomes negative and surly I have learned to say, "Mr. D, I'm not talking to you. When Dave shows up you have him let me know and we'll finish this conversation." Dave nods his head, acknowledging D's presence and that usually stops Mr. D in his tracks.

~

There is absolutely no argument that what I said to David that night in the restaurant at the Marriott is accurate. Depression was much worse than Parkinson's disease for me. Unfortunately, PD, for him, is still a bitch.

The second surgery and its aftermath became complicated. The surgeon and the neurologist, two men we both liked very much, found me in the surgical waiting room, their faces downcast. "We had to end the surgery before we could test the stimulator on Dave. He was very uncomfortable during the procedure, kept complaining about his left arm hurting, and he got aggravated with us. He wasn't cooperating. He actually got fairly testy and kept moving his arm and complaining. He even put that arm behind his head when he was awake and we had to re-sterilize the field."

"Oh my, he always does that to relieve the pain in that arm," was my alarmed explanation.

"He shouldn't have done it during the surgery!" They were pleasant to me but I could see the strain in their faces from a long, trying operation. "We ended the surgery early and could not get feedback from Dave on whether or not the stimulator was in the correct place. But the computer readings on the implant were excellent, so we went with the numbers and expect that his result should be good, but we don't know for sure."

"When can I see him?" was about all I can recall mumbling to them as my concern for him and the outcome of the surgery rose. It was to have been so easy this time. Not so.

In the recovery room, I found him with his head entirely shaved and wrapped in gauze and his eyes closed in obvious discomfort. He blurted out, "This was the worst experience of my entire life!" David, not one for such superlatives, unknowingly frightened me due to how he was speaking about what he had been through. "I heard every word that was spoken among the surgical staff when I was supposed to be 'under,' even hearing the surgeon tell the resident to be careful not to cut into my brain as he used the saw to cut through my skull."

"Surely, he was joking."

"Yeah, I guess, but it wasn't fun to hear. And then I contaminated the surgery site by putting my hand on top of my head."

"Yeah, I heard about that from the doctors."

"Well, lying there so long on a hard flat surface made it hurt intensely. Since I was out of it, I didn't really know what I was doing. I put my hand up there to stop the pain. Boy, did I get into trouble. They were mad." The sedation that was meant to put him into a loopy fog for the initial part of the operation just didn't work the same as the first time. Then, they had called him from the mist and asked him to give feedback on his tremors or pain. This time, he really had been aware of much that went on in the ER instead of being in a pleasant place in the recesses of consciousness.

"I even heard the docs talk about stopping the surgery, unfinished. When I heard that I gathered whatever awareness

I had of what was going on and decided to suck it up so they could finish. There was no way I wanted to go through that again, ever!"

"I'm so sorry, Davey. It's over now, so let's be glad about that." I kissed his cheek.

"Good thing too, because if the first surgery had been anything like this one, I never would have gotten it again. And look how I'm shaking."

He was shaking—a lot, a whole lot—on his right side, the side already helped by the first stimulator. This should not have been. I asked the nurse, "What's going on? Shouldn't he not be shaking?" He was very uncomfortable.

The recovery nurse reassured us. "It can take awhile for the stimulator to begin to function normally after being turned off during the operation." Okay, we accepted it even though this had never been his experience before when the stimulator was turned off, and then on again. The tremor had always stopped within seconds. When Dave was taken to his room for the night the tremoring turned into what I would describe as violent and non-stop. Again, we were told it would calm down. David looked more miserable than I had ever seen him, suffering from the effects of the surgery that, understandably, had drained his stamina. But with the shaking, too, he was in a disturbing condition. No one could help him. More than one nurse, seeing the bandage on the right side of his skull, said, "Of course you're shaking, Mr. Derr, you just had the surgery and the stimulator's not turned on yet."

"But that was for the left side. My right side already had

DBS." He tried to repeatedly explain but lost his patience when the nurses didn't even seem to understand the right and left brain crossover, a basic of neuroanatomy. "Idiots!" Dave said when they weren't around. His frustration with those dolts mounted and my attempts to get them to understand made no difference. He asked for a doctor, for someone, anyone, to check him. A resident did come but the answer was the same.

I looked at my spouse and watched our future play itself out in his body. The electro- stimulators' influence only lasts an unknown number of years before PD progresses to a point where their effectiveness lessens. Someday they would cease to help him.

Less than three hours post surgery, his arms and legs were shaking so much that the bed seemed rocket-fueled. His right leg rocked six inches or more at a time. He had a "just shoot me" look on his face. The next day his neurologist turned on the working stimulator from his first surgery and, of course, his tremors on the right ceased immediately. He had gone through a night of misery and little sleep simply because they'd *forgotten to turn it on*. We were not pleased but understood it as an inadvertent oversight.

That long night, however, we both had thought that the new surgery had undone all the good of the first one. At one point, when a nurse came in to check his vitals, I kissed his cheek and told him I was going out to look for some tea. At the end of the hall, I entered the visitor's lounge. In all my years of hospital calls to see members of the churches I've served, I had never seen such an uninviting, cold waiting room. The walls were cinder block, painted in what had become a dirty off-white. The furniture was sparse, industrial vinyl upholstery with metal legs and arms. There were no windows and nothing on the walls; only a sad arrangement of dusty silk flowers on a side table adorned the space. I sat alone and tried to call a few people from my cell phone to update them on his condition. Reception was bad, so I gave up. Then I began to pray.

"No one is there to hear you." It was not said aloud, yet, I heard it clearly in my mind. In that instant, through doubt, I lost God. I knew it was not a normal kind of doubt. For a religious person, doubt is the first cousin of faith. Why else call it faith? In fact, doubt is necessary to help faith grow. Theologian Frederick Buechner wrote, "Doubt is the ants in the pants of faith. It keeps it awake and moving." I like that quote since I have enjoyed asking God-questions and looking for answers. Despite my doubt, I always "knew" there was a God.

No, this was different. In that cold Cinder Block Room, I was certain God did not exist.

Dunking My Head Underwater

S*urely, I did not really "lose" God. Is this a fluke? Am I just tired? This cannot be. Have I really been wasting my life on total BS?* Oh, the turmoil in my mind.

During the weeks following Dave's surgery I lost a lot of sleep, rising most mornings at 4:00am to plead with God, hoping I had been wrong about God's non-existence. My tuxedo cat, Wyatt, would join me on the sofa during my sometimes tearful pleas, but never God. Weeks went by. I led worship, preached sermons, and continued my pastoral duties of visiting the sick and praying with them. All without faith. Hypocrite was my new middle name. I didn't like being a phony. More than that, I missed God desperately.

I decided my best chance of spiritual renewal was to follow certain threads backward. I thought the key to unlocking my faith crisis might be gaining clarity and insight from my past. I harbored hope that such an investigation would help me find God again—if there was a God. I felt truly alone in the universe. Dave could not relate since he was religious in order to support me, not for himself.

I always thought I knew loneliness. It has been an overarching aspect of my life as a pastor. In a congregation, I help to create and support a community of faith-based people. But I can never truly be a part of that community. The proverbial "It's lonely at the top" has been my experience, even though I have been atop relatively small organizations.

For example, early in my ministry, I attended a baby shower for a church couple with whom Dave and I socialized. The guests, the majority from the church I served, arrived first and we all watched expectantly at the windows for the mother-to-be to arrive. Spirits were high, the group making jokes and teasing each other. Unexpectedly, the husband arrived with his wife, but in separate cars. A guest said, "Oh, separate cars, they must be getting a divorce." We all laughed at the absurdity of the comment as we watched the mother-to-be, sheltered by her husband's arm around her shoulder, waddle across the street. At least, *I thought* we had all laughed.

Immediately, the nearby grandmother-to-be looked at me, aghast. "What a thing for you to laugh at. You, a pastor! I can't believe it."

"It was a joke!" I tried to respond, but the woman continued to *tsk, tsk* as she moved away from me to the door to welcome the couple. This was not the first time I had been berated for not being what another thought a pastor should be. I withered inside, realizing I could not be myself, even at a baby shower.

I felt sorry for myself whenever I was criticized for showing a small glimpse of my irreverent (normal) side. Note to self: *hide that part.*

Alienation was also part of my interaction with non-church people. Once new people—neighbors, people I met on vacation, folks in an exercise class—found out I was a pastor they treated me differently. They'd apologize for swearing, make excuses for drinking a beer, even deliberately turn around when they saw me approaching at the grocery store. My mere presence made people feel guilty and I surmised it was due to an image many have of a pastor as conservative, judgmental, and accusing. I am none of those things, but I seldom had a chance to reveal my progressive nature since folks did not give me an opportunity to befriend them and show them who I really was. I knew things about the lives of my neighbors because I would ask questions and take an interest in them, but it was often not reciprocated.

Once, when my daughter, Lynn, was hospitalized for two weeks as a teenager, the neighbor who knew about it, whom I had reached out to when he had had back surgery, never acknowledged our plight. His neglect is one of many tales of people crossing me off the list of possible friends because I had "The Reverend" in front of my name.

Consequently, as the isolated CEO at church and the neighbor with "judgmental clergy blight" oozing off of me, I found that lonesomeness was part of my life. I am gregarious and somewhat bawdy by nature. By being ordained I unknowingly sacrificed the potential to have many friends in my life.

Once, when I interviewed for a job as a parish pastor, after all the church and theological questions had been asked, the interview committee surprised me with their final question. "What is the most difficult thing for you about being a pastor?"

"Not being able to be a normal person," was my quick reply as I told them of a woman who had recently reprimanded me for wearing gray nail polish when I was preaching. "It looks good on me," I said and they laughed. (My nails are royal blue as I type this.) I didn't get the job. They gave it to a man who crashed the attendance by half within his first year. They could have had me, but they went with a man who turned out to be jerk. Sigh.

Yes, I had few friends. I came to accept this as part of the clergy life for me. I was unaware of how the isolation I felt was taking up residence inside me in the Cinder Block Room, aiming to squeeze God right out of my life. But up until that day, God had been a "refuge and strength, a very present help in time of trouble" as noted in Psalm 42. When I was on the curb outside Dr. Hunter's office, I believed that God *was* there while I cried. God listened. Jesus was my companion. I can count on my husband to accept me just as I am. God, too. It meant everything to me to feel deeply known by my divine friend. The Cinder Block Room took that surety away from me. I was adrift on a raft, heading toward what I thought to be atheism, and did not want to plunge over that falls. It would mean, I expected, not only the annihilation of my career, but also of me.

From my earliest memories, Christian faith and the

guidance I derived from it had always been threaded through my life. One Sunday when I was a preschooler, my family was snowed in so we could not get to church. My mom sat in the living room with me and my three siblings and gave us our own private, fun-filled Sunday school lesson…When I was six I began to sing in the children's choir. I loved it when we (the choir) would leave our seats and proceed to the steps in front of the altar, face the congregation, and sing our little hearts out. It was moving even for one so young…As a teen, I joined the youth group and found it a safe place to be, where I did not get teased. I experienced my first kiss there while playing spin the bottle and even learned to play poker. While on a weekend youth retreat I had a first-time mystical spiritual experience that both baffled and thrilled me. During prayer time, while I was sitting cross-legged in a recliner, I began to cry. I looked around and saw others doing the same. These were not tears of sadness, but a wash of joy mixed with a what-the-heck-is-going-on sensation. It was an odd, exciting, and spontaneous God-moment. The adult leaders were glowing with happiness that it had occurred among us. It served to validate my trust in God.

That childhood faith matured and had guided my thoughts and decisions as an adult. I had been ordained nine years when, on July 19, 1989, my father died. He was only sixty. What a robbery. His dark hair had not even grayed yet. The pituitary gland tumor that had almost killed him when he was forty-two had grown back. In 1971, the whole experience had been extremely frightening since he was in the hospital, blinded, without knowing the cause. What would happen to him, to us, a family of six, if he could not see? Thankfully, three weeks into that crisis, the tumor was discovered and surgically removed. Some of his sight was restored, but not enough that he could drive. Following recovery however, he could still work as a concrete company dispatcher and thus was able to help support his family.

I, the eager teenage driver at that time, often got to pick him up and drive him home. He'd give a cheery wave to his buddies at the plant—the place where he could swear, the place where he did not mind being called Herbie—and load his chubby body into our used car. The confines of the drive always eased us into conversations. I had always liked my father, but I *really* liked my new father. The idea of death, hovering so close, had changed him. "I think they took part of his brain out when they did that surgery," was my mother's glad remark as she observed the happy-go-lucky person that her husband of twenty-two years had become. It was remarkable.

Gone was the angry man who had often pounded on his bedroom floor with random items to get us four kids to turn down the sound on the evening television show. Gone too was his depressed, tired demeanor. He continued to be a portly man with a handsome pompadour hair style, but he became the proverbial jolly fat man, never forgoing an opportunity to be silly or pull a prank. His effusive joy was infectious, especially with the three grandchildren he lived to know. They adored their Pop.

My dad went into the second surgery waving to my mother

saying, "See you soon." We thought the advances in laser surgery over the past many years would surely yield a positive result for him. But it was not to be. "With the first surgery, we gave him eighteen years he would never have had," the surgeon told my distraught mother. "I'm sorry we could not do it again. He's had a stroke and is likely blind. Recovery is not likely." My father never spoke again. Mom remained at his bedside until his death, three weeks later. My journal from that time recorded how my faith assisted me in this loss.

> *Dad died, a struggle of a death as his lungs conked out and he labored to breathe. My prayer is that he knew the presence and love of his family in his last minutes. He couldn't talk since the surgery so it bothers me that he must have felt so alone, unable to communicate with anyone. Yet, Jesus was with him, of course, so that makes me glad. He wasn't really alone.*
>
> *In many ways there is part of me that is apart, observing how I handle this. I'm sad, yes, but trust that God knows what's best. Perhaps he would have been blind and an invalid had he lived. That would have been such a burden for him and Mom. The observer me is surprised at how easily I really do accept that he is resurrected and with the Lord. I really do believe this Christian stuff and it's a strong faith! Observer me is surprised at that.*

My father's death had tested my belief system. I came through it questioning why God did not heal him, but never doubting God's existence. Certainly faith had defined me. It was a foundation I shared with millions of people. But millions do not become pastors. Why did I?

~

In 1974, I was in my sophomore year at Bloomsburg State College in Pennsylvania and had changed my major from speech pathology to "undeclared" which is college-ese for "I have no freaking idea what I should do when I grow up." Having been directed to the career counseling center, nineteen-year-old Margie was embraced by caring people who wanted to help her make a choice for her future. They introduced me to examples of career profiles that might guide me. The notion that my likes and dislikes could actually assist me in my choice of a major was new to me. As one who always excelled as a student, I knew I could ace just about any course I took (except maybe calculus—egad!). I was being asked to consider that acknowledging the things I was passionate about and did well might help to guide me toward a fulfilling career.

My "What I Like or Am Good At" lists included the following things: singing, acting, studying and getting good grades, reading, marching in parades in color guard, working with kids, helping others, Jesus, knitting and crocheting, sewing, being a loyal friend, teaching, musical ability (piano and the $50 guitar I was learning to play), and, if I admitted it, taking charge. My mother had told me that I was "bossy."

My two younger brothers, who I had tormented with my self-righteous pronouncements about how to improve their lives and characters, will attest to my controlling ways.

Although the career center never asked for them, the opposing list of "What I Don't Like or Am Not Good At" would have included: things that reflected my issues with my body image or appearance, and an unsettled feeling about my chances of getting married. I was five foot seven and weighed 122 pounds; I still do. "Weiss, you are so skinny you could fall through a crack in the floor," was the middle school taunt of my peers. My breasts were 34 A's and barely filled a bra. "Beanpole," was the term that followed me from elementary school into high school. Genetics had deprived me of four teeth (one was missing from each side of my central/front incisors). Thus I had two holes in my top row of teeth, *and* two holes in the bottom. I learned how I looked to others when just a ten-year-old. Assorted kids would laugh and whisper loudly enough so that I could hear them. "Buck teeth. Gap tooth!" Despite the fact that in eighth-grade my orthodontist had corrected the malocclusion (that had made my teeth push my upper lip out in buckish profile), he had also moved my eye teeth over to fill the space on top, which ended up leaving me looking vampirish. But I was still toothless in the bottom spots. The plan had been to someday fill in the bottom missing teeth, but that required money, which my parents did not have. Is it any surprise that I disliked having my picture taken and always smiled with my lips together? When I was in junior high I wrote in my diary, "I'm so ugly. No boy will ever want to be with me." My father had read it and tried to convince me otherwise. At the time, I didn't know whether to be mad at him for that invasion of privacy or glad that he was trying to boost me up. As my father was not a boy my age, his words did not soothe me. I think his love did though.

When I was in high school I believed that my teeth, small breasts, prudish ways, and that I got good grades kept me from enjoying my teen years in the way that I had always expected I would. I'd grown up reading *Archie* comics. My life then was certainly not an *Archie* comic. I'd only had two short-term boyfriends and I'd had to wait until I was an elderly seventeen for my first kiss—Dan Lambert, with tongue. It was nice and so much better than practicing on the pillar that stood as a divider in our living room. I was also heartbroken that I did not have a date for the senior prom. I had to settle instead for going to the post-prom-all-night bowling party, which I had loudly proclaimed (to anyone who would listen) was better than getting all dressed up anyway. I didn't even fool myself.

Archie, Jughead, Reggie, Veronica, and Betty were always dating, hanging out at the malt shop, or enjoying adventures in hotrods. There was no teen hangout in my small town and I was seldom invited to parties due to the aforementioned prudish tendency and, I always figured, because I was not pretty. Drinking, drugs, and premarital sex were "wrong." My small crowd of girlfriends did not dabble in such things and hence, we ranked about number five on the one to ten popularity scale—not total losers, but not part of the in-crowd either.

Hence, when it came to picking a new major in college there were some things I could not consider from my "What I Like or Am Good At" list. I could not be a professional singer because of my teeth, thinking only in terms of a singing career making me highly visible. I pictured a television camera doing a close up of me. Ugh! Acting was out too, for the same reason. Marching in parades while spinning a rifle in drill routines (my favorite high school activity), would hardly pay any bills. Nope, I had to pick something practical that I could do no matter how I looked, and since no one would marry me anyway…

I also truly believed that God had made me smart for a reason. I had been fourth in my high school graduating class and felt an obligation to do something worthwhile with my brains. (Idealism should have been added to my positive list, but I'm certain I was unaware of that characteristic back then.) I wanted to make my life count and therefore began to contemplate some sort of church-related career. My experiences growing up in a Lutheran church had shown me that the seasons of parish life lent themselves to teaching, singing, and acting, while including ample opportunities to work with children. Perhaps I could become a Director of Christian Education (DCE) in a parish, a traditional female role that did not require beauty, just dedication and a love of Jesus. I had both. I changed my major to sociology. Learning about group interaction and behavior would be a good foundation for graduate school at a seminary.

So that's how I decided to go to seminary. Nevertheless, I realized my decision to not go for DCE but become a pastor had roots from far earlier, way back to a summer day in rural eastern Pennsylvania. The year was 1958. I was four years old. My six-year-old sister, Susie, our father, and I were "swimming" in the Manatawny Creek, down the hill and across the meadow from the circa 1800s farm house called Dingley Dell in which our family of six lived. The water was only about two and a half feet deep, even when dammed with a row of stacked rocks, so Dad was actually wading. I was only about three feet tall, so it was swimming to me, and I loved it. We were never allowed to go into the creek without Daddy, and we sisters knew that Mommy would never go in there lest she get her hair wet, so when the warm days came and Daddy was game for it...delightful.

The sun reflected off the water into my eyes as I watched the silhouette of Daddy pulling Susie up by her arms, about to dunk her into the water, but she loudly screamed in protest. "No, Daddy, I don't wanna get my head underwater. I'm scared, I'm scared!" Despite Daddy's assurances that she would be fine, Susie vehemently refused, so the two settled for him swirling her through the gentle currents.

"My turn, Daddy, my turn!" As he negotiated his way toward me over the slippery rocks and mollusks on the creek bed, my voice rang out the competitive challenge that would define my life. "Dunk my head under the water!" I wanted to be different, better than my sister. My arms were raised. He grabbed both my hands, lifted me up and brought me down into the water, sloshing me thoroughly. As the bubbles burst around my submerged head, I was mildly frightened but was determined not to let it show while I gamely held my breath.

When he pulled me from the deluge I arose triumphant and brave because I had been better than my sister. "Again, again," I cried as Susie watched from a few feet away. None of us were aware that I had been symbolically baptized, reborn as a scrappy, can-do, highly competitive individual. Later that day, Susie, two-year-old Stevie, baby Timmy (in his high chair) and I gathered around the supper table with my parents. While we had been wading, Mommy, still svelte after bearing four children, had been in the yard digging up young dandelion plants. She put the steamed dandelion greens, covered with hot bacon dressing, on the table next to the chicken she had plucked and roasted after my father had slaughtered it in the backyard that day. My sister would not try the dandelion, but I did.

I have been seemingly fearlessly dunking my head under water my entire life, taking risks and walking "the road less traveled by." Robert Frost's poem, "The Road Not Taken," concludes that such travel "has made all the difference." Was it a misstep for me to go the less traveled course in life, choosing a previously male-dominated career? In my ongoing ambivalence about my cursed and blessed life I cannot help but conjecture that my days would have been happier had I taken the well-traveled road, walking with the pack of traditional women. In fact, it is more than wondering, it is a perception, or perhaps a fantasy, that people who are not clergy, i.e. who are "normal," have a much easier and contented life.

Yet I wonder if, in the twenty-first century, any vestiges of traditional women's roles have survived. In a college sociology class I learned about the prescribed roles that were part of a seventeenth century Puritan family. It was stipulated that men were the heads of the family, in positions they believed were defined for them in the Bible. Women and children were to be obedient to the divinely chosen men who were the hunters, bread winners, and chief judges and authorities in family life. Women had clearly defined tasks, beneath men, oriented around the household responsibilities of cooking, making clothing, quilting, preserving food for the winter, and of course, child-rearing. This, too, was seen as their God-given place in life. When the professor asked the class who would have liked to have lived in Puritan society, I was the only one who raised my hand in the affirmative. The class looked at me as if I had been transported in time and was wearing the white bonnet of a Puritan woman. I quickly explained.

"Women in those times knew what was expected of them. They didn't face all the choices that I do. There's something appealing about the simplicity of the clear expectations for the women as they planned and lived a life." At least this is how I like to remember the incident, that I was lucid, while in reality, I know I stumbled through my explanation, trying to relay the conflicted feelings that were tumbling around in my subconscious. Translation: I was afraid. Afraid of the choices before me, since I was still mired in a I-have-no-freaking-idea-what-to-do feeling in my life. A Puritan woman's role seemed so simple. I liked to cook. I was an accomplished seamstress, having expanded my skills since my first project, an apron, in seventh grade home economics class. I could produce a crocheted or knitted sweater easily and enjoyed the creative process. Both were things I had challenged myself to learn. My mom neither sewed nor did needlework. Was I a do-it-yourselfer from the wrong time?

Additionally, although embarrassing for me to now admit, at that stage of my Christian evolution, a man telling me what to do and being "head" over me, was acceptable. The Bible said so, I was told. It must be true, right? Today, the conservative Christian concept of "headship," that men have a divinely given status of authority over women, makes me want to gag. I have moved beyond—way beyond—interpreting scripture in such a narrow way.

So how and why did I go from being a young co-ed, frightened of a future of too many choices, to a woman who entered seminary to train for a traditional male job? I know now. Because Little Margie had once cried out, "Dunk my head under the water, Daddy!"

There have been forces that have conspired to form my personality. These laughing schemers were the birth order gods, capricious deities who rubbed their hands together as they plotted who I would become due to the kismet of being a second born. The Weisses epitomized the baby boomer family: four kids conceived and birthed in five years during the decade after World War II when scores of couples were doing the same. The day I picked up Kevin Leman's *The Birth Order Book,*[1] I flipped through the pages wondering how this man had spied on the dynamics of my family, how he knew me. Ding, ding, ding! Clarity about myself, my sister, and my brothers abounded on the pages.

Birth order. This is what I learned: second borns like myself are often competitive by nature since as children they have a tendency to feel inadequate in comparison to the older sibling. As young children, Susie and I could have both drawn a picture with crayons and, of course, being drawn by the older artist, hers would have looked better than mine. Even if my stay-at-home mother praised mine, I would have seen that Susie's was superior. My brothers, into adulthood, comment with some good-natured derision about how competitive I was/am while playing board games. Leman showed me why I had asked to have my head dunked that long ago day. As a typical second born child I lived to catch up, like a horse chasing a carrot on a string. The manner in which I did that is classic second born stuff: by being competitive and having the desire to achieve. This desire became my ruler. Is it the curse of being a second born? It's the driving force that has helped me excel and succeed, leading me to becoming an independent thinker, willing me to do things differently, and to take risks. Oh, the risks I took.

"Are you crazy?" numerous people, mostly church folks, said to me in 1985 when they learned that I was planning to travel to South Africa and Namibia on tour with a Lutheran group. I was thirty-one and had been ordained for five years. Legalized racial segregation, apartheid, was still in effect in both countries. In Namibia, my travel group would be in a war zone where the people were fighting to oust the occupation forces enabling South Africa to control Namibia.

"Oh, I'm not worried. It'll be a great adventure." And it was. I got arrested in Soweto, along with my tour group, because our group of mostly white folks being in that black ghetto was seriously suspicious to the police. It was oddly exciting to spend the afternoon at the jail, awaiting word as to whether or not we were to be thrown into a cell. We were not, since they finally decided we were harmless tourists. A few days later, I unexpectedly preached at three worship services because "a lady pastor" was a must-see for the Lutherans there from several different tribal groups. My hastily written sermon was translated into three languages, sentence by sentence, as I delivered it. In Cape Town, I met Desmond Tutu who had won the Noble Peace Prize the year before. Grand. Those three-and-a-half weeks of travel are a highlight of my life.

"Are you crazy?" numerous people said to my husband and me when we decided to adopt an older child. "You're gonna have a lot of problems. I know someone who…" and then the well-meaning person would tell us a tale of doom regarding adoption gone wrong, meant to dissuade us from this choice. "You'll regret it. Can't you have children of your own?" We didn't know as we never had tried—conception that is. (I once knew a pastor's wife who told me that when she was pregnant a member of the church wondered how she had gotten that way as he thought pastors did not have sex. He must have once been a Catholic.) Eight-year-old Lynn entered our lives in 1987 and yes, those soothsayers were right. It was hard. It was hell. But it was also joyous. It was a blessing. I'm proud of all three of us and the fact that we moved from simple make-it-though-this-day survival to love and deep connection.

So it seems that taking the risk to enter a male-dominated profession obviously suited me. However, I am not only a second born, competitive risk-taker, but I'm also a middle child. According to Leman, middle children grow up feeling squeezed and rootless. Those are loaded words. As soon as I read them, insight abounded. Peering back through the six decades of my life, the continual longing I have had for community, one that I have never really found in church, stems from that rootlessness.

Here is how "squeezed" worked itself out in the Weiss family. I felt squished between Susie, who had naturally gotten the most attention from my parents, as firstborns do, and Tim, the baby of the family, beloved by all who adored his cute antics. Poor third born, Steve, and I lived the middle-child blues in the family. We found our bliss with our peers. Steve was a star athlete and had a host of friends who were at the house regularly. He fit what Leman explained, "The squeezed out middle child goes outside the family to create another kind of 'family' where he or she can feel special."[2] I did that by being the kid who liked to join groups. I played hockey—terribly—for two years in high school. I played basketball—terribly—for three years. Both groups gave me a feeling of belonging. Marching in the band front with the color guard was a better match, although the bus trips to parades meant I had to watch all the other girls making out with boys when I was boyfriendless.

Rootless? For me, rootlessness exhibited itself in a subconscious impression that I did not fit in. I was pummeled by the middle-child forces and felt bereft and alone. I recall when I was a nine-year-old swinging on the backyard swing, saying out loud to the universe, "Susie is the apple of their eye and I'm nobody. They don't really love me." Interestingly, Susie now tells me she would think, "Nobody loves me!" Childhood angst for us both. The birth order gods laughed.

Nevertheless, I *was* developing positive life characteristics: the aforementioned risk-taking behavior and independent spirit. Unaware, however, of these favorable things, I sought a way to be noticed. I became a scorekeeper, one who utilizes the practice of keeping mental lists about your own or someone else's good points or flaws. Scorekeeping became my ruler.

It began in first grade, November 1960. I was a new student transfer since my family had moved from Dingley Dell to small town Oley, Pennsylvania, where Dave also grew up. I now know that a middle-child demon was alive and well in my six-year-old mind as it coached me with whispers in my head. "You don't really fit in at home, so here you are in a new class where you also don't fit in. So how are you going to show the teacher and kids that you're a valuable little girl? Here's how. Keep score and come out on top."

It didn't take me long to figure out how to do it. One day we had a spelling test and I felt anxiety rise since I didn't know all the words. We hadn't covered those words at my other school. I solved my dilemma by cheating. I looked on another student's paper. I got an A and the teacher praised me in front of the whole class while the other kids looked at the new kid with what I hoped was awe. Now I was not just a new student; I was a *smart* new student. I made sure I would receive that affirmation again and again by studying my spelling words, my arithmetic, and whatever else first-graders were taught. School for me became a competitive person's chocolate. I sailed through first grade with straight As. That sealed my identity for the next eighteen years. I continued to look at others' papers if I thought I needed to, ironic since I knew it was wrong and really not necessary. Grades became my "ultimate concern" which theologian Paul Tillich uses as a metaphor for a person's god. It was the way for a homely, lonely kid to feel good.

That little scorekeeper began as a Cradle Lutheran. My parents, Herbert Weiss and Evelyn Leid Weiss met in the late 1940s at a Luther League, the name at that time for a young adult club of Lutherans. Herb was seventh of nine born to farmers; Evelyn was the middle child of three with a factory machinist father and a registered nurse mother. Dissimilar in background, Herb lived in rural Berks County, Pennsylvania, while Evelyn lived fifteen miles away in a suburb of the city of Reading. The commonality that brought them together and led to their romance was church. After their marriage in 1950, it was natural for them to continue to be involved in a local congregation.

The children: Susan, Marjorie, Stephen, and Timothy, all

brown-haired and slender, were born respectively in 1952, '54, '56, and '57. We were each baptized within the first months of our lives, and mine was on October 31, 1954, (Reformation Day) when I was six months old. On that day, a pastor poured water over my bald baby head three times and intoned, "In the name of the Father, and of the Son, and of the Holy Spirit." That ritual is a ceremonial washing and initiation into Christian faith. Marked with oil on the forehead in the shape of a cross, the bapitzee is called to "Let your light shine so people may see your good works," and hence be pointing toward God. It is meant to set the course for a child's life. It does not always. With me, it worked.

My parents were not "C and E" Christians (those who attend worship only on Christmas and Easter) nor were they "Hatched, Matched and Dispatched" people of faith (those only in church for baptisms, marriages, and funerals.) We worshiped every Sunday as a family, the four little Weisses dressed in our church shoes and outfits, often being plied to quietness by cherry lifesavers and coloring books.

Church worship of the 1950s and 60s was not kid-friendly, unlike in the congregations I have served as the pastor where a Children's Sermon is part of worship: children come up to meet me near the altar and we sit on the floor together while I, in five minutes or less, present a simple one-point lesson to the inquisitive and often talkative kids. Adults tell me it is often their favorite part of worship, which may not be saying much for my adult sermons! I call the children by name and enjoy the opportunity it gives me to interact with them. My final reward comes later when the huggers of the group come up and wrap their little arms around my legs.

"This is for you, Pastor Margie," a four-year-old boy quietly but proudly told me one Easter day as he gave me a chocolate bunny he had gotten that morning. "It was all his idea, Pastor," his mother told me. "It was the only one he got." My heart got mushy and I made sure I sent him a thank you card to encourage him in giving to others.

However, in the congregation of my youth there was little opportunity for any child to interact with the pastor. I knew our pastor, Reverend Speaker (his actual last name), to be the old man who stood up front in the church. I envied him because he also got to climb the steps into the pulpit, the mysterious place forbidden to children. He stood high above the congregation to preach. Sermon time was when the cherry lifesavers were a must, as was a pen so I could doodle in the church program by filling in all the Os, Ps, Bs and Ds in every word.

My weekly interaction with the pastor was in the receiving line after worship. I endured the way he spoke to me in baby talk and the accompanying cheek pinching and head patting. (I make sure never to do either of those things to the kids at my church.) That was about all I knew of a pastor's job. Until...

"I bet you can't get this stone over there." My next door neighbor Mary Ann's freckled face was radiant with the challenge as her red curls blew around in the wind. I had walked home from my first-grade class and then met with my sister and other neighborhood kids who had gathered in front of our house to play "Throw the Stone into the Puddle," a game we had just invented because of the puddles that beckoned to us after the quick May showers.

Main Street, Oley, as usual, was not busy. Oley had one main drag and two side streets so we thought ourselves safe. But it was exciting to be a little daring in our game. We were on one side of the street with a pile of stones and the puddles were on the other. The aim of the game was to throw a stone across the street and get it directly into a puddle and make a splash. It was muddy fun.

Our mothers were visiting in Mary Ann's house and without saying it, we knew that we had a short window of playtime before they would come out and shoo us off the side of the road and spoil our fun. "I got one!" Mary Ann was excited to have made another splash, while my throws weren't far enough to land anywhere near the puddles. All the other kids had done it but me. Embarrassed, I looked around for more ammo and found an old dog bone. Brilliant! Much better than an old rock.

"Watch this! I'm gonna get this bone in the puddle." I tossed it, noting what a good missile it was since it was lighter than the stones. I actually overthrew it.

"Look how far that went," one of the boys yelled.

After hearing that, I was determined to use the bone's unique flying style again. I looked both ways, up and down the street, to watch for traffic just as I had been taught, and then skipped my skinny self across the road to retrieve my bone. "I got my bone. I got it! Just wait and I'll get it in the puddle for sure."

Bone in hand, I started back across the street and then

things got wacky. To this day, I don't exactly know what happened. A car hit me, but it didn't knock me over. *Did it really hit me?* I actually took a few steps towards my house. *Where did it come from?* I tried to run. The man driving the car shouted to me. "Lie down, get down!" How strange. *Why can't I just run home?* I heard the screams of my sister over those of the other kids. The man shouted again, so I took a few steps back and obediently lay down in the street. The faces above me—Mary Ann, her brother, the strange driver, some people I had never seen before—looked weird and the voices didn't make sense. Everyone was talking at once. I started to cry, not because I was hurt, because I knew I wasn't, but because I was scared. I should have looked both ways.

The driver lamented, "It's a good thing I was slowing down to make the turn. I saw her but didn't expect her to dart out like that. I sure hope she'll be okay." The circle of heads above me nodded their agreement as I sniffled. When I saw my parents kneeling by my side I full out wailed. *What have I done?* No one would let me move, even when I insisted I was fine.

Dr. Grimm, a white-haired man smelling of rubbing alcohol and soap, arrived along with his usual brusque manner. "Why hasn't anyone moved this girl off the road?" The crowd murmured that they thought they shouldn't move me and he shook his head and reprimanded anyone listening for letting me lie on the road. I never did like that man. Soon enough I was in the back seat of our station wagon, my pixie-haired head in my mother's lap, quietly crying as my dad drove us to the hospital where I spent the next two nights "under observation" lest I had a concussion. This was 1961, my stay a sharp contrast to Dave's one-night stay after his brain surgeries years later.

I was as mortified as any seven-year-old could be that my hospital bed was a crib. *What do they think I am, a baby?* In the large ward, there were other beds, regular beds, with other kid patients, boys, and girls. They weren't in cribs. Nevertheless, I wasn't lonely even when Mommy was not there with me, and the kids in the beds didn't seem to think the crib was terrible. What an interesting adventure it was as I listened to the older girls and heard their stories about why they were there. One had an odd dried up umbilical cord type thing hanging from her belly which she gleefully showed me as she stood on her bed and raised her shirt. It was wondrous and grotesque.

Being hit by a car seemed to impress them and I embellished the details to make it much more exciting than it had really been. They also liked the attention I received when Pastor Speaker came to see me. I was mystified, however. *Hmm, what is he doing here? I thought pastors only worked on Sundays.* That phrase has been said to me repeatedly through the years as a joke, one that long ago lost its humor, but as a child, I really thought that was the case. He talked to me about the accident, inquiring about any bumps. His baby talk wasn't so annoying this time. "My, you are a brave little girl, Margie. I'm so glad you're okay."

"Yeah, but they have me in a crib. I don't like it."

"Well, don't you worry. I won't say a word about it. I know

you're a big girl. You *are* a first-grader, right?" I nodded my head. "See, almost grown up I'd say."

Before he left he said a prayer for me. I felt special. I had learned something about pastors beyond the cheek pinching and sermonizing. *Pastors make people feel special.* I liked that. Maybe one of my brothers could become a pastor.

At no one time did I ever question the men-only pastor rule. I did wonder why only boys could be acolytes, the Lutheran equivalent of a Catholic altar boy. Stevie and Timmy were able to wear a special robe and light the candles on the altar for a worship service. When told it was a boys-only job, I accepted that the church world operated in that way. I observed the women of the church occupied with service projects. They took up collections to send kids to camp and sent items to needy kids overseas. It was men, however, who ran the place. Only men were ushers, those who solemnly strolled down the center church aisle in two pairs to get the offering plates from the acolyte to hand out to people. Men were the leaders on the Church Council. It showed me that church was a man's world with women and girls as helpers. It seemed normal and I accepted the status quo.

Our congregation got stirred up in a good way when a new pastor came to town: enter Jim Papada, a young guy in his thirties. I thought he was intriguingly different despite his out of style crew cut in that Beatles age and his cigarette smoking. (Even in the "Winston tastes good like a cigarette should" era, I thought smoking was really disgusting.) After his arrival, things at church began to change. Women, for instance, were elected to serve on Church Council without the patriarchal roof falling in. I liked him from day one.

Like turned to mild adulation when he gave us junior high kids confirmation instruction, which is a two-year series of classes to teach young teens about faith. I had questions about God and looked forward to getting some answers even if it meant reading dry textbooks on the Father, Son, and Holy Spirit.

A year earlier, in sixth grade elementary school, fellow Lutheran, Kathy, and I would hang out together regularly during recess. Neither Kathy nor I wanted to go on the swings, play kickball, or have the boys look up our skirts if we were on the monkey bars. (Girls could not wear pants to school.) So Kathy and I would walk and talk, pondering the complexities of life. One day the topic was creation.

"If Adam and Eve were the first and only people, who did their children marry?"

Kathy immediately understood the dilemma. "Yeah, what about that? How can that be?"

"But we're not really from Adam and Eve because the flood destroyed everyone except Noah's family, so who did they marry? Must have been each other. Yuck."

"Yuck for sure. Can you imagine having sex with your own brother?" We both reacted in mock horror at the image.

"I just don't get this stuff about creation and the flood. It doesn't make sense at all." Kathy agreed. Our conclusion was, "If the Bible said it, it's true." A voice inside told me I was a fool if I bought that. A theologian was being formed. I never spoke to my parents about my questions, since faith was not something normally discussed in our weekday life, an irony for a church-going family that I did not note until years later.

There is true and then there is truth. Fast forward to confirmation class in which I was introduced to thinking differently about Biblical truth. I was a very excited girl the day Pastor Papada talked to us about Adam and Eve being *symbols* for all humanity and not actual historical people. "It's a story to try to tell us the truth about God and about ourselves, but it's not a true story."

"What truth?" I asked, confused but intrigued.

"If you look at the story you'll see that when the couple ate the forbidden fruit and God found out, the man blamed the woman and the woman blamed the snake. Humans do that, you've done that. We don't take responsibility for our own wrongdoing and often try to blame others."

"But what about the truth of God?"

"Well, even though Adam and Eve had sinned, God still cared for them, giving them clothes and a new place to live. This shows how the writer wanted to convey that God never gives up on us even when we do our worst."

I could have kissed him! No one in my little town was happier that day than I. What a relief. The concept that one could interpret a Bible passage and not just accept it blindly captivated me. I had had my first theological light bulb moment. I didn't have to throw my brain out the window to be a Christian. I was so excited that I talked to a number of my friends about it, none of whom seemed to understand my enthusiasm. No matter. I was thrilled.

I was a smart kid, but when it came to understanding the basic message of Christianity, I was dumb. I did extremely well in school mainly because I had a good memory and could regurgitate information. Processing that information—not so much. My church taught Christianity primarily using "faith language" which I've come to know was, and *is* inadequate. Churchy words like justification, grace, sanctification, and redemption sound very weighty and reverent. However, most people don't know what the hell they mean.

My first preaching professor at seminary forbade us novice preachers from using such churchy words unless we defined them. And if we described them with a Webster's Dictionary type definition he chastised us. "Don't you dare use the word 'justification' unless you tell a story in your sermon that illustrates what justification is. The same goes for any of those theological jargon words. Stories communicate the faith. People can identify with them and will often have a moment of clarity as they listen, thinking, 'Oh my gosh, that's me! I get it, I get it!' That's what you aim for in your preaching," he continued. That's how God will knock them over with love or kick them in the ass. Stories can change the listener. Jargon words are boring as hell."

I most certainly grew up hearing the jargon words and did not understood what they meant. "Jesus Christ died for my sins," is a common Christian missive, but I had no freaking idea what that really meant. I knew it had something to do with getting to heaven, but my youthful understanding of Christianity was not close to the core of actual Christian faith.

I believed God to be the creator who loves people as the supreme creations. God lived in heaven and wanted people to live there with him after they died. (God to me was always a him in those days.) If you were good while on earth, heaven was the ice cream sundae for a job well done—a payment, but even better, a reward. If you weren't good, then you would die and GO TO HELL! It was all afterlife-oriented. My preferred destination was heaven, so I was as good as good could be. What a wonderful challenge it was for my competitive proclivities to climb that ladder of good works and niceness. How easy it was for the scorekeeper in me to judge the kids and adults around me. I was able to know—really know—that I was better than them. Heaven for me, hell for them. The scorekeeping I did in school easily transferred to how I understood God at that time. God was the eternal scorekeeper.

However, the embryonic theologian in me worried. *You're only being good with the ulterior motive of getting to heaven. Hypocrite! Your goodness is not pure since you're just thinking of yourself.* If only I had understood what those jargon terms, salvation and grace, meant in terms of Jesus' life and death, then maybe I would not have been so off the mark in my deductions. However, throughout the rest of my high school years, I continued with my blithe Goody Two-shoes faith in which I saw myself as better than so many.

Early in college, fundamentalist Christians had entered my world and had given me a story to help me understand Christian faith. It was great. For awhile. But it did not last. Let me explain.

In the spring of 1976, I was nearing the end of my senior year of college. I had done well in my sociology major and had just found out that I was to be the valedictorian of the School of Arts and Sciences at my college. As I walked down the campus hill toward my dormitory, a warm spring breeze was blowing over the red tulips and yellow daffodils that lined the sidewalk. It was a glorious day and I was feeling quite proud of myself. I was the validated valedictorian! Finally, after years of academic toil to prove my worth, I was going to get the recognition I craved.

Then, he was walking toward me: Gordon, the dreamy guy from the fundamentalist Christian fellowship group I'd once been part of, which was simply called, Group. Tall, lanky, and sandy-haired, he was my "type." I had lusted after him in my daydreams. I reacted to the blond god before me with an intake of breath that I let out slowly in a longing sigh. I had often orchestrated the seating arrangements at Group meetings so that I could sit near him, even following the lead of some other girls who would cry during prayers. Whether their tearful prayers were genuine or not, I noted that it always got a nearby guy to offer a comforting hug or gentle shoulder rub.

My dewy-eyed reaction to prayer was a mix of true emotion toward the God I had come to rely on, as well as a convenient tool to get attention from Gordon. However, my prayer tears never got more from him than a quick squeeze of my arm. Gordon, you see, wound up dating the prettiest girl in the crowd, which of course made sense to me at the time. Handsome and beautiful as a pair was a universal given.

"Hi, Margie."

"Hello, Gordon." I tried to be casual.

"I'm glad I ran into you. I need to ask you something." He was so serious, his searching eyes angry, but for what reason, I could not suspect.

"Oh, what's that?"

"I heard that you're gonna go to seminary to become a pastor. Is that right?"

This was a tone I recognized. Superior-man-over-lowly-woman tone. I'd heard it from another guy from Group who had been upset two years earlier because I had knitted during Bible study night. He'd said I was disrespectful, that high-and-mighty jerk. I was multi-tasking before there even was such an expression. And now, here was Gordon, sounding like him. I mustered my confidence and said, "Yeah, I've been accepted at a Lutheran seminary in Philadelphia."

"You know that Satan will use you in many ways if you become a pastor."

My blond god fell from Mount Olympus into a pile of fundamentalist bullshit. Fundamentalist Christians generally interpret the Bible literally, differing greatly from what I had learned from Pastor Papada. Gordon was among those in Group who said the world was created in seven days. I had asked at that time, "What about the dinosaurs?"

"I don't think about them." It was a blond moment for him.

Well, I did think about them and accepted the reasonableness of evolution and the science that supported it. Evolution seemed an exceedingly more interesting and more God-like way to create, rather than the quaint stories from ancient writers. That was one of the reasons I had left Group after sophomore year. Yet, I was surprised at his Satan analogy.

Gordon quickly got to his agenda. "There are other paying jobs you could do in a church without being a pastor." He was going to sway me over to the "truth," I observed.

"So...why do you say that? And why are you so interested?" I was already expecting the answer I would get.

"The Bible *clearly* says that women should not hold authority over men. If you try to do that you'll be the devil's tool." His eyes narrowed on me with an I-know-the-mind-of-God glare. If I were to have received a thousand dollars for every time in my ministry someone has used the term "the Bible clearly says" to uphold their own prejudicial opinion, I would be wealthy by now. Not to mention that many things in the Bible are just not clear.

I was offended and countered with what I hoped was confidence. "Lutherans don't interpret the Bible like that. We take into account the culture of the times. I considered Christian education work, but I really feel God is calling me to be a pastor."

"But it's wrong, wrong, wrong. You're not following God's voice, but your own." This he said with great authority. I have witnessed other people do that who are convinced that an unfathomable God has revealed certainty to them. I, on the other hand, have more and more questions about God the older I become and never presume to be absolutely clear about many God things. "Love people, help them, care for the earth, and leave a legacy of a better world" is as certain as I can be.

Gordon's challenge did unsettle me. I had considered the possibility that I was heading to seminary due to my Need to Be Recognized Nerve, the same one that had been tingling happily over the valedictorian notice not moments before. I could not believe that the devil (if there is such an entity) was behind my decision, but I did contemplate whether my own desire to achieve did not, indeed, skew my thinking. I knew I was just trying seminary for a year, unsure of the validity of a "calling," but Gordon was not going to find that out from me.

"You know, Gordon, this is one of the reasons I stopped attending Group. Too judgmental and self-righteous, kinda like you're being right now. It's really unkind of you to speak to me like this."

"Just loving you in the Lord, Margie. You really should consider that most Lutherans are not saved. Believe me when I say that you'll make trouble going against God's plan like that." He smiled.

As he swept by me he gave me the supreme brush-off for those of his ilk. "I'll pray for you." That never meant a kindness as in "I'll pray for you because you're ill," or "I'll pray for you to do well." This was the old "I'll pray for you because I know you are going to hell" prayer. I had become well acquainted with this priggish form of religiosity in Group.

My affiliation with Group had started out cheerily when, as a freshman, I attended an evening meeting to see whether this Christian fellowship group would be to my liking. It was. We sang every week—folk songs with guitar accompaniment—and I enjoyed the topical discussions about how to live my faith as a student. Soon enough I bought a guitar and a chord instruction book and taught myself to play. My first song used just three chords, E minor, A minor, and C. The tips of my fingers hurt a good deal until calluses developed from repeated playing and singing of "They'll Know We Are Christians by Our Love."

Love is what I initially felt at Group, where God unexpectedly showed up in my life in a new way. Theological jargon words, the things that had kept me from "getting" Christianity, were replaced with stories about faith that moved me past the scorekeeper God to a God of love. The story that finally explained "Jesus died for my sins" to me was so simple.

> A forest ranger was walking in a newly burnt out section of forest, heat still rising from the singed ground and trees around him. At the base of a tree was the charred carcass of a bird with its wings spread out, not unlike a cormorant drying its wings. He kicked it aside thinking sadly how it symbolized the destruction of the fire. Immediately, there was movement underneath that body. Four baby birds squawked out their presence. Their mother had hidden them under her wings to protect them from the flames, offering her life for theirs.

A light bulb of recognition burned brightly in my conscious thought. Suddenly, I knew this Jesus. "He died to save you," said the red-headed female guitarist whose guitar skills I was trying to emulate, "loving you just as the mother bird did. He died in your place. And once you are saved, the promise of that sacrificial love lasts into eternity. You live for God now and later, forever in heaven."

I ate it up. I no longer had to *earn* God's love; it was simply there, through Jesus. All I had to do was stay connected to Jesus and I would be "saved." Saved from what? Of course, they told me: sin, death, darkness, but most of all, hell. Salvation was all about the afterlife.

I dove into it like a fish on a line, not realizing that getting hooked meant being pulled out of the waters of real love into the Lake of Despair where Gordon sailed his ship. I was saved because I knew Jesus. Group told me that those without that knowledge or "decision for Christ" were headed to a fiery afterlife. Were my parents saved? I wrote them a letter to find out if they had really asked Jesus into their hearts, worried that they would not be with me in heaven. Their response was in the affirmative, but still, I worried since they did not seem to fit the "saved profile" that Group espoused.

Being initiated into this Christian worldview, in which a person had to choose Jesus as personal savior in this life or go to hell in the next, led me to more questions than answers. How could it be that Jews were definitely on the train to hell, as were Buddhists, Muslims, Hindus, most Catholics and, just about every Lutheran? Anyone who said they were Christian but had been baptized as a baby (Catholics, Lutherans, Episcopalians, and more) was sure to burn in hell because you had to *know*, according to fundamentalists, you were being baptized. How could babies know and choose Jesus as their personal savior? My parents did not fit this, nor did I. In my nuclear family only my sister conformed to this standard of salvation since she had been rebaptized at age eighteen in the Baptist church of her soon-to-be husband. It was great for my sister and led her into a life of faith that nurtures her to this day. However, it caused great heartache for my mother who viewed it as a rejection of her own faith. How could I forget my mother's hurt and do the same thing to her?

The waters of the Lake of Despair were flowing over my toes and up into my life and I did not like it. I began to question if "Believers Baptism" was the only possible way to be a true Christian. I also bristled against the checklist for determining the saved from the unsaved. Among the things on many, but not all, fundamentalist Christian lists of dogma were:

- Every word in the Bible comes directly from God.
- The world was created in seven days.
- Adam and Eve were historical people who were in a garden with a snake that talked. They ate from the Tree of the Knowledge of Good and Evil and thus ushered in the "Fall of Humanity."
- There was a world flood with only Noah, his family, and some animals saved from it.
- Evolution was wrong.
- At the end of time, Jesus would break into history and "rapture" away the faithful, floating them up to heaven.

- All premarital sex was wrong.
- Homosexuality was always sinful and a perversion of God's plan for men and women.
- If your life did not show the Fruit of the Spirit listed in the New Testament book of Galatians (love, joy, peace, patience, kindness, goodness. gentleness, faithfulness and self-control) you might not really be among the saved.
- Any person in the whole world who did not accept the formula, "accept Jesus as his/her personal savior," would go to hell.

A favorite television series of mine from the 1990s was *The Nanny*, a situation comedy revolving around a widower, Maxwell Sheffield, with three children. He hired a beautiful woman with a unique hypernasal voice that was like fingernails grinding on a chalkboard. Her child-rearing methods were most unorthodox, but effective, so that the troubled household was healed of grief. Fran Fine, the nanny, was usually up to some harmless scheme that led to the boundary between employer and employee being crossed. The plots evoked *I Love Lucy* of old and were hilarious. The sexual tension between Fran and Maxwell would occasionally move them toward kisses, while both usually denied their increasing affection for one another. Fran obviously loved him and he, her.

Mr. Sheffield, however, kept Miss Fine at bay, always apologizing for his inappropriate behavior, leaving Fran, who enjoyed the amorous clutches, dangling like the proverbial fish. In one episode, when Fran and Maxwell were on a plane that seemed to be crashing, Maxwell declared his love for Fran. They kissed passionately. The studio audience wildly applauded. Finally!

In the next episode, having been saved from plane crash death, Maxwell "took back" his profession of love, saying it had only happened since he thought he was dying. Fran's emotions were trampled. The comedy writers twisted Maxwell's testicles to the great delight of viewers from then on for being such a cad. Took it back!

Group was my Maxwell Sheffield, telling me God loved me unconditionally and then taking it back with all the rules and "yes-buts" they laid on what I determined was theological poop. In the end, Maxwell finally came around and firmly declared his love for Fran without taking it back. Such repentance would never come from Group since it was I who had to conform to their definition of faith or be labeled as among the unsaved.

I could not stay with Group and so I finally stopped attending. It was a good decision affirmed by my mentor, Pastor Papada when I had told him of my foray into that very different type of Christianity.

Two years later, I watched as Gordon strode away from me in his happy cloud of self-righteousness. Certainly, I was now assuredly among the unsaved as I did not embody his matrix for a Christian woman.

Nevertheless, I will always be grateful to fundamentalist Christianity and my conservative Christian friends and family members for helping me to understand the jargon word, "grace." One does not have to earn acceptance from God. It just is. I still find much among the fundamentalists that appeals to me: I like their devotion to Bible reading, the uplifting praise and worship songs, and their ability to discuss faith openly, something shy Lutherans do not do easily. The judgment of others however, based on their not fitting the "formula" is just not love. I shake my head in sadness regarding it.

My Alter Ego

On the day in 1976 when Gordon tried to correct and shape me, I was unaware that I was happily trying to fit myself into another ill-fitting mold, that of becoming an acceptable wife for the man I loved and intended to marry. I had gotten engaged during my senior year of college. Yeah, I was surprised, too. After the dry years of high school dating, I had been flabbergasted to discover in college that I was not as unattractive as I had assumed. No way was I a guy magnet, but somehow men were able to see past my teeth issues and lack of cleavage—at least enough to date me.

And so, I was relatively inexperienced with men, my dance card having been filled with first-and-only dates. There was Sam who took me to a frat party where I got drunk for the first time on grain alcohol punch. Cool! I liked it. Terry had a very large nose that was a turnoff to me. What, can I say? I was young and superficial. Jamie was a sweet guy who took me to the movies and, aside from his body odor, it was pleasant. When I said yes to a second date, hoping he just hadn't had time to shower after baseball practice the night he took me out, my friend Teri said, "More power to ya. I wouldn't want to be with a guy who stinks!" And stink he did on date number two, so there was never a date number three. I made out with Greasy-Haired Nameless Guy in his van after he picked me up at a college dance. Dumb, yes, but I was flattered that he wanted to be with me. I still remember the kisses and the thrill mixed with revulsion that I was actually doing that with a guy I had just met. Of course, I now recognize how I had set myself up for possible date rape, but such a term, and education on how to avoid it, didn't exist in the seventies.

When I was a freshman, I put myself into an extremely vulnerable position again. Mr. Barker was one of the faculty advisors for Group, a role that engendered trust. He set the bait and I took it. Just a few months into my college debut I had attended an evening meeting with Group that included singing the Christian folk songs that I liked so much. Mr. Barker approached me for conversation. "You're a good singer," he complimented me. A short man in his forties, his receding hairline and pompadour made him look like a cross between my father and Bing Crosby.

"Why, thank you, but I didn't pass the audition for college choir."

"Try again, Margie. You should make it." After more requisite pleasantries he asked, "Have you ever been on a plane?"

"Nope, I never have."

"Well, lucky for you I'm a pilot and I have my own plane at the airport here in town. It's a four-seater that I plan to take up Saturday. Would you like to go for a ride? I like introducing students to flight."

His offer sounded fun and irresistible to me; a new adventure to be had. "I'd love to, Mr. Barker. What time?"

"I'll pick you up in front of your dorm at 10:00am. I look forward to taking you up for your first ride."

That Saturday the sun colored the inside of the cockpit amber as Mr. Barker took the plane up from the small Bloomsburg airport. I was surprised there were no other students along for the ride but was not at all apprehensive as we ascended, just fascinated with the new experience of seeing the many hills, buildings, and the rain-muddied Susquehanna River from this sky view.

I enjoyed the landscape as we talked about his flights to his summer home in Maine as well as campus life. "In a small plane like this I can fly much lower than jets do and you can see the land below without clouds getting in the way." After about twenty minutes he loudly cleared his throat. "Say, you've never taken any classes from me."

"I'm not a business major, Mr. Barker. I'm taking mostly general ed classes right now, but I know I don't want to major in business."

"Too bad. A pretty thing like you could go far in the business world."

"Pretty, me? I don't think so. I'm kinda average."

"Well, I only bring the pretty ones up with me. Now, you're not nervous are you?"

"Not a bit. This is cool." I was also extremely naïve.

"Are you sure you're not nervous?" He placed his right hand on my left knee when he repeated his question. He did not remove it. My fun, first flight turned creepy. What was I to do, trapped two miles high with this lecherous man? Shoulda-woulda-coulda still fills my mind as I think back on my bewilderment at that moment.

"Ah, no, I'm not nervous. But, I need to get back to campus for play practice. Thanks for the plane ride, but I can't stay up here much longer." What a liar I was.

"Oh, too bad. I was looking forward to showing you more." I bet he was. Thankfully he removed his hand so that he could bank the plane around but then returned it to what had become my clammy knee as he guided the plane towards the runway. Why did I not ask him to move his hand? Fear? (I taught my own daughters when they were young the difference between good and bad touch, but I don't think I emphasized that it could happen when they were older as well, as it did for me.) I'd never had to be assertive with an adult before. I guess I felt powerless. After the plane came down without incident, I had no choice but to get in his car for the ride back to campus. In this pre cell phone era, there was no way for me to get in touch with anyone to be rescued. He drove more slowly than I thought was natural. "Say, would you like to go out for dinner with me next week, Margie? I know a restaurant outside town that I think you'd like. Great steak."

"Uh, would your wife know we're going?"

Even from the passenger side, I could see his eyes rise in anticipation. "Why no sweetheart; it would be just you and me." This Christian man was a snake!

"No thank you, then. I wouldn't feel comfortable doing that. You're married." My words were as pointed as they could be to one whom I still needed to rely on to get back to campus. Thank God, Centennial Hall was ahead. "Just drop me off right here. I can walk back to my dorm." I scooted out of the car and, taking the steps two at a time to escape, did not look back as he called me sweetheart again. My dorm friends were suitably grossed out and afraid for me when I told them my flying tale. I reported the incident to no one in authority since I was not aware that Mr. Barker had made the ethical breach of sexual harassment. That term was not yet part of the regular lexicon. I ignored him when I saw him at Group after that, continuing to feel stupid and betrayed by someone I thought I could trust. I didn't know that this first betrayal by a Christian (and a teacher no less!) was one of the foundation cinder blocks in that room I would encounter more than thirty years later. Insidiously, that room was being erected through my negative experiences with Christians.

Adventurous, I surely was, but was also such a trusting innocent. In my handful of dates, I remained a "good girl." No premarital sex. No drugs. Very little drinking. I remained secure in righteousness, accompanied by a large dose of judgment toward many of my peers. I observed them having young adult experiences, "learning lessons the hard way," while I resembled those Christians in Group who acted morally superior, whom I eventually dismissed as misguided. For example, a fellow student I knew from Group seemed to have an inner wild child that came out when away from the influence of her church and parents. She partied often and when I found out that she was having public sex while other students were around to observe, I was appalled and judgmental. She, a part of my Christian fellowship group, was acting like that? I'd thought our values were the same. Morality was showing itself to be a multilayered peculiarity. Good people sometimes do bad things, I surmised. She eventually stopped when she realized that the guys were just using her for sex when what she wanted was a relationship.

A relationship was what I, too, desired: to fall in love and have a man love me back. It was a simple, normal goal but one I kept in a secret place in my soul. One evening before I was in college, I was drying dishes while my mother washed. I declared, "I'm never getting married. Who has time for that? That way I can do what I want, when I want." That bravado was the cover for my worry that no one would ever want to marry me. Still, I hoped. That hope bloomed to reality when I began to date Aaron. We had been in high school together, but were only casual acquaintances. Close to six feet, he was slender and blond with muscular legs due to his long distance running. I loved light-haired men, comparing them in looks with handsome actor Robert Redford. Aaron's attractiveness was somewhat masked by the dark rimmed, out of style glasses he wore, but his soft-spoken manner was appealing.

In the summer of 1972, before we became a couple, we had just graduated from high school and joined a busload of people from the Lutheran churches in our area to assist in cleanup from flooding caused by Hurricane Agnes. The city of Wilkes Barre, Pennsylvania was devastated. At the time, Agnes was the most damaging hurricane ever recorded, having killed 129 people as she made her way from the Gulf of Mexico northward, dumping heavy rainfall on the Mid-Atlantic states. We had each paid our own way to go on that goodwill trip.

The day is easy to bring from my memory. When we arrived we were shuttled to a downtown residential area to assist homeowners. I stood on the street and looked up at the three-and-four story row homes and saw the graying, muddied lines left by the water, which had reached the rooftops. I could not believe it. But I was not there to gawk. Soon enough I was in someone's home, scraping wallpaper from still-damp walls and carrying out trash which sadly contained life treasures that could not be salvaged. It was a meaningful experience for my eighteen-year-old self. It was useful, grown-up type service. That satisfaction through helping others influenced my later decision to be ordained since the call to do justice and serve others is part of the Judeo-Christian heritage, and continues to be an essential aspect of my worldview.

On the trip home, although we had not worked together that day, Aaron and I sat together. We knew each other from shared high school classes and had been passing acquaintances. It was a get-to-know-you bus ride. We had just graduated and we talked about our fall plans. He was to attend a

Lutheran-affiliated college in Allentown, Pennsylvania, while I was heading farther north for my studies at Bloomsburg. Aaron was a PK—Preacher's Kid—his father being a pastor in a church in the rural hills outside Oley. Our common Christian background was appealing to me, and, as I found out much later, to him as well. Aaron had always seemed personable to me, but was a bit on the shy side, so our conversation on the two-hour bus ride home was an unveiling of facets of him that I could not have imagined. He was funny but exhibited a responsible seriousness about life that I now understand (that Leman!) was due to his first born position in a family of four boys. I was surprised by him. As the bus bumped along, I tried to indicate my "liking" to this boy, by making sure my knee would bump against his from time to time. Sadly, my knee did nothing to attract his attention.

I thought little of Aaron for the next few years until we both wound up having summer jobs as playground leaders at play lots in Oley; I was the female leader of a male-female duo at one school, and he was the male leader at another. Coordinating joint activities brought us together and our casual friendship slowly, surprisingly, became much more. It was thrilling—my first long-term relationship and the first time I was in love. When I knew that he loved me too, I was transported to an emotional sanctuary. He loved me. He loved me just the way I was. I fit someone. Teeth and breasts be damned. Aaron loved me.

One day that summer, I returned from a shopping trip feeling sheepish. "Aaron, you'll never believe what I did. I was driving to Nichols Department store to get new fish for my aquarium and I was thinking about you."

"That sounds good."

"Yeah, I was so happy. Joyful, I guess, and daydreaming about our future, so much so that I realized I was going the wrong way, heading into the mall instead of Nichols. I must have driven seven miles before I noticed."

"That was kinda dumb." I looked at him, expecting a smile. "You gotta pay better attention." No smile. He was not pleased.

"Uh, okay." I was hurt and mad, but said not a word. This should have been my first clue that all was not what it seemed in Margie-Aaron world. I did not express my anger. Not healthy.

I've tried to retrieve positive memories of that madly-in-love time of my life but oddly, most of it is gray with only bursts of color. Gold was the color after we had not seen each other for several months while apart at our colleges, and I recall the sighing peace I felt when in his arms at our reunion. Red characterized our make out sessions and what I can quaintly call "heavy petting" which was exciting and new. Green permeated the day when I watched him run a cross-country race and then run into my arms at the end, sweaty and happy. The gray, however, is pervasive and it has puzzled me. I don't remember our first date, nor our first kiss, memories of which are still quite vivid from not only my husband but also a few other men whom I dated. I barely recall places we went together or what we did. How can this be? I surmise it is because Aaron was not dating Marjorie, i.e. me, he was dating Pretend Margie, the person I thought he wanted me to be. I remember very little of the good times in our two years together because they are the memories of that pretender and not mine. I do remember the grays, which border on black, in the negative emotions they can sometimes arouse.

I deemed our relationship strong and blissfully perfect because we never fought. One day he was trying to teach me to drive stick shift in his yellow Volkswagen bug, the one he cutely said ran on chipmunk power, with the little critters spinning in a hamster wheel to move the car. When I could not get the clutch out smoothly to a make a left turn across traffic I blurted out, "Shit!"

"You don't need to talk like that," he sighed as he reprimanded me.

I didn't counter with the truth that "shit" is my favorite swear word, that I usually say it in triplicate, and when really necessary, five times. Instead, I made a mental note to hide that part of me from him.

Aaron was not a TV fan. When he stopped by my house to visit I made sure I turned off the set before he came in, lest he know that I had been watching. And there's more. One day during our second summer together, he stood in the kitchen at my parents' home and watched me make sandwiches. I made them as my mother and father always had, with a layer of butter on each piece of bread followed by the mayo and then the meat and cheese. "Why are you putting butter on that? It's not good for you, you know. You should stop doing that." I verbally agreed but was annoyed with him. I knew I would continue to put butter on my sandwiches when he wasn't around if I wanted to.

Later that same day, while sitting on the back stoop, I told him of the odd dream I'd had the night before in which I'd had sex with my father. "Isn't that the weirdest thing in the world, Aaron?" Neither of us had any experience with intercourse, for we had agreed to a waist-up policy for intimacy. I assumed that the conversations that had led us to that decision meant that we could talk about anything sexual.

"Why would you tell me about that dream?" He scooted his body about a foot away from me. "It's very inappropriate."

"It was just a dream. I can't help what I dream about!"

"Well, keep it to yourself." Humiliation burned through me. I mentally added this to the list of things to keep from Aaron. No sex dream talk. No butter on sandwiches. No TV watching. No swearing. And no telling him that I did not like his eyeglasses. When he told me he had ordered new glasses, I was really looking forward to the change from his dark, horn-rimmed specs to something more up-to-date, but the new ones were almost identical to the old. I lied and said they were nice.

Was this love? He was a good man, in excellent physical shape from his long distance running and attention to his diet. I admired his devotion to that discipline as well as to his family and to God. He had long-term goals about where he wanted to go in his future career. And we never had a fight, a good thing, right? Just after New Year's Day 1976, soon before we were to return to our respective colleges to begin our final semesters, Aaron asked me to marry him. Pretend Margie happily said yes while Marjorie watched horrified in the background, aware of the suicide represented by the engagement ring. We picked out a simple ring, set a date for the following year, and blissfully anticipated the day, knowing that it was to launch us into a wonderful life together. I was madly in love with him. I was also caught up in madness.

~

Pretend Margie had blinded me to the unhealthy aspects of my relationship with Aaron. However, thirty years later I would deliberately call her up in order to seek help with surviving my crisis of faith. This time, she was my friend, the one who helped me function in my job. I want to explain how she did that.

It was September 2010. I was in my office at church one evening when there was a knock on my door. "Can I talk to you? Is this a good time, Pastor?"

"It's fine, Hillary, what's up?" The normally charming and magnetic Hillary was not exuding her usual perkiness, something that often drew others to her. She was on a break from church choir practice and I could tell she was troubled.

"I was at a Jewish New Year's dinner the other week with my husband and some of our friends. After the blessing over the food, the conversation turned to God and one woman said, 'I don't believe in God.' Then it seemed that more than half the people at the table agreed with her, that they did not believe in God either."

"I can tell this really bothers you, Hil. Your face shows it."

"That's why I wanted to talk to you. It really does bother me. In fact, it hurts me. How can they not believe in God?

Why did they just have the Jewish blessing for the meal if there is no God? I don't get it and I guess the best I can say is that I'm hurt and bewildered by my friends' and my husband's religion. I'm not sure why it hurts me but it does. Is this common among Jews?"

"Not sure, but I do know that the Holocaust changed many Jews in their beliefs about a God of love. And you can be Jewish by culture without being religious. I guess those people might fit that profile."

"I suppose so. It really bothers me, though. I would never be able to live without God. Oh, I hear the music, gotta get back to rehearsal. Thanks, Pastor. I knew you would understand." She breezed off with a grateful smile.

I would never be able to live without God. Yes, I had empathy with Hillary's emotions. I'd been deep in my struggle of faith in a God entity. Hurt and bewildered? That seemed familiar since it was a just over a year since my Cinder Block Room experience and I was daily pondering the question about the efficacy of prayer while wondering if God "is." Yet I continued to search for some shadow of God that might grab my life. My faith was like a balloon slowly losing air and I was trying to stop the bleed before we were flattened.

I had been devouring books about faith and doubt. In one night at a dinner, Hillary had learned more than she wanted to know about her friends. But for me, the skirmish within my heart seemed a war because it was connected with how I made my living. *I'm not sure I believe in God and I'm a pastor.* As I watched Hillary leave my office I thought, "Imagine what that's like for me." The choir began to sing and I went back to my research for my next sermon.

Considering my doubts, preaching weekly was paradoxical but not that difficult. I'd been doing it for over thirty years so once my research was done, I could crank out a six-page sermon in forty-five minutes, whereas in my early days of preaching it would sometimes take me ten hours or more of sweat and struggle to develop a message. Sermons are meant to be "God's proclaimed Word." I always take the task seriously, and overall, enjoy doing it. To know that my words can influence whether or not people choose to contribute to charity, mend a relationship, or influence how they raise their children, are the most fulfilling aspects of being a pastor. Could God still do that through me? I seemed to be falling off the faith cliff into an abyss that was telling me I was a fraud. And so, Pretend Margie helped me pretend. Maybe she would make it stick.

Over the years I'd developed the gift of preaching. Fredrica, one of the pastoral interns I had supervised for a year, agonized over the preaching task. "I'm stuck again, Margie. Can you help?"

"What's your theme? Which Bible passage are you basing it on?"

Once she had told me her plan, I could quickly relay to her things she could use to bring it to life. "How about the TV commercial about…Or the recent movie about…In your own life story, perhaps your recovery from your accident would fit…"

Fredrica, a vivacious second-career seminarian, although older than I, guilelessly looked to me for guidance. In other words, I knew she wasn't sucking up to me when she said, "Margie, you amaze me in how easily you can see a sermon and how to use story to make it flow. Wow!"

Consequently, despite my ongoing religious doubts, I could still deliver a sermon that had punch. "You made us cry again, Pastor." "What a message! I'm going to tell my friend to listen to it on the church website." "Your sermons are why I kept returning when I first came here."

Pretend Margie's existence had been a detriment to my emotional balance all those years before. However, post Cinder Block Room, I clung to her. She knew what to do to portray faith when I needed that public face. She kept me going from day to day, assisting me to act like the Christian I once was and hoped to be again.

Now, back to Aaron and Pretend Margie. It was the fall of 1976, just three months after college graduation, and Aaron had taken a job as a teacher in another state. I was "trying" seminary in Philadelphia for the first year of what could become a four-year Master of Divinity degree program toward ordination. My fiancé was supportive as I followed what we both thought was God's hand guiding me. We planned to marry the following June 1977 then figure out our next move from there.

Why was I just "trying" seminary? I had never seen a woman pastor before. I had no model for what I might be getting into.

While still in college I had gone to Pastor Papada a number of times to discuss my consternation with the conservative Christianity of Group. He helped me see that I needed to disassociate from them. Later, I spoke with him about my idea to get a master's degree in religious education so I could be a Director of Christian Education at a large congregation. "Why not become a pastor?" he asked.

I was taken aback. "Ordination. I can't imagine it. What a crazy idea."

"Not really. Lutherans ordain women now and you just might be a good pastor." His eyes were alight with the possibility. "I saw you in confirmation class. You took to theology. Still do."

"Really?" I threw my head back and laughed while scanning the religious items and certificates on the wall of his office. "This is nuts. You really think I could do what you do?"

"It's worth checking into. I can set up an appointment with a pastor who helps guide people who are thinking about seminary. He can tell you the procedure and expectations."

"Okay, let me talk to Aaron about it and I'll get back to you." And so it began. The seed was planted.

Society was still in great flux regarding women and their changing roles. The 1960s of my childhood had brought the civil rights struggles and protests against the Vietnam War, later to be seen as cultural transformations. For example, I marveled when black faces and black families appeared on television commercials as advertisers took off their "Whites Only" signs, just as the South had been required by law to do. The Vietnam War led to my young adult generation questioning the government's moral compass after it embroiled the United States in what seemed an unwinnable war against the elusive specter of communism. I had worn a POW-MIA bracelet honoring a colonel lost in the war. He never came home; I found his name on the Vietnam War Memorial wall.

Civil rights and war protests, coupled with growing women's liberation, and the sexual freedom seemingly created by the Pill, put the United States on a metamorphosis in fast-forward. Federal laws improving the economic status and rights of women were passed. My denomination was greatly affected by these social stirrings, as female and male voices were beginning to advocate for the ordination of women to the position of pastor. Hence, when Pastor Papada suggested I become a pastor, I remembered a dialogue in a Sunday school class I'd attended just before there was to be a national vote to ordain women at a convention of Lutheran representatives from around the country.

"A woman pastor? Why would a lady want to do that?" One of my father's peers, Mr. Wayne's, eyes crinkled with amusement at that thought.

"I agree, there're plenty of things women can do in the church like teach Sunday school and lead the youth group," the president of the congregation's Lutheran Church Women group concurred.

Another gentleman added, "Pastors should be men. After all, Jesus was a man. Women need to take care of the children or stick with being teachers and nurses."

Pastor Papada had come to this forum prepared with mimeographed handouts of Bible passages regarding the role of women in the early church. "You can see from the passages in St. Paul's letters that he was sometimes in favor of women leaders in the churches he founded but at other times, against women speaking in a public setting. Our wider church is in the process of deciding which of Paul's voices to follow."

Dorothy Peter, the always-laughing mom of one of my youth group friends, drew the participants' attention to a quotation on the handout. "I like this passage from the New Testament book of Acts." She read it out loud. "In the last days, God says, 'I will pour out my Spirit upon all people. Your sons and daughters will prophesy. Your young men will see visions, and your old men will dream dreams. In those days I will pour out my Spirit even on my servants—men and women alike—and they will prophesy."

Pastor Papada summarized, "Yes, it seems to be saying that God gave the same abilities to men and women."

Dorothy agreed. "My best Sunday school teachers were women and I bet they could have delivered a good sermon. In fact, I think the church would benefit from women clergy."

Mr. Wayne good-naturedly sneered at Dorothy's suggestion. "Well, all I have to say is that if a woman is standing up there in the pulpit I wouldn't be able to think of anything other than her sex life. And if she were pregnant, that would be a deal-breaker for me. No way am I in favor of this."

Despite Mr. Wayne and others like him, my denomination at that time, The Lutheran Church in America, voted in

1970 to allow the ordination of women, a move that led some people to walk out of the national assembly when the motion passed. Others at that assembly rejoiced that the church had taken a step to practice what it preached in its theology of God's love and grace for all people, grounded of course, in not interpreting the Bible literally. Hence, that the Bible says "women should be silent in the church" (I Corinthians 14:34) was now seen (in the seventies) by many as a cultural directive for early Christians, not God's word for all time and eternity.

My parents were among those who questioned if I knew what I was doing when I told them I was thinking about entering seminary. Initially I, too, had dismissed the idea. Women pastors were so new among Lutherans, after all. Then I opened the newspaper and saw an article on clergywomen. Later, a magazine featured clergy couples. *If they can do it why can't I? I have the skills. I love God and the church. I agree with Jim Papada that I'm a budding theologian. Okay, God, I get it. This should be an adventure.*

I was willing to boldly go where few women had gone before. (Yes, I love *Star Trek*.) Aaron was lovingly agreeable to it. My siblings were mystified, I believe, but my parents just wanted me to be happy. "So you really want to do this seminary thing?" Dad asked me. "It's not gonna be easy for you."

"Dad, you know I get good grades all the time. I figure God gave me these brains for a reason. I think this is why: so I can serve in this way. I want to make the world a better place."

Seminary Wow, Parish Ministry Pow

I joined about fifty students, at least a third of them women, as the entering class at the Lutheran Theological Seminary at Philadelphia, LTSP, in 1976. Life there for me was much better than college. The campus was small and buildings were stone with an old-world charm. I lived in a co-ed dorm for single students—men and women together not only in the common areas but also sharing joint bathrooms at the ends of the hallways—how delightfully different it was from my previous women-only dorm with restricted visitation hours for men. I developed an easy friendship with my assigned roommate, Mary, who remains a friend to this day. Her sense of humor kept me light when I got too serious and competitive. Because LTSP was located in the city, I enjoyed the opportunity, on a student's budget, to take the train downtown to go to city things like concerts, museums, clothing stores, and historical landmarks.

It was a stimulating life change from rural and small town life. I missed Aaron but found my time taken up by my classes: Introduction to New Testament, Church History, and Basics of Pastoral Care. Our phone calls and letters to each other continued in much the same way as they had when we were separated by being at different colleges, and of course, the ring on my finger promised a future together.

I got a campus job waiting tables at the dining hall to help pay for my tuition. It was the perfect job for social me since the dining hall was the hub of community life for the campus. Professors, students, and visiting scholars often dined together there. As a waiter, I got to schmooze with everyone as I served food and coffee. I got to know fellow students, welcomed visitors, and overheard stimulating conversations on theology and church.

I also learned very quickly that this was not a staid and uptight place. Off-color jokes were de rigueur. (I think students didn't want to appear overly stuffy.) I told such jokes well. The campus gossip mill functioned effortlessly. It was said that a person could sneeze on one end of campus and someone on the opposite end would say "God bless you." Information about students and professors spread rapidly as well as legends from the past and rumors from the present. A student some years before had apparently killed himself by throwing himself in front of a train because he was a homosexual. A certain professor was an alcoholic. Another had a photographic memory and could tell you on what page a random reference was in a book. I was experiencing "community" in a way I had never known and found it heavenly. Yes, heavenly, since I believed God had brought me to this expansively open and diverse community of people who gathered daily for worship, and were bound together by faith.

My dorm companions and I would spontaneously do outrageous things. When we first-year students were studying for our Church History exam, the upperclassmen and women in the dorm orchestrated a party in honor of the author of the lackluster text book used for the course. The party entailed putting on a costume representing a church history character and going from room to room inviting people to a party in the Pit, the sunken living room for the entire dormitory. What fun. I was animal lover St. Francis of Assisi in a robe adorned with stuffed animals.

Even better was this: one early evening a few friends and I were visiting in my classmate Bruce's room, discussing the movie *Animal House*. "Toga party!" Bruce shouted as he sprang up from the floor and ripped the sheets off his bed. Soon enough, we all ran to our rooms to do the same, wrapping ourselves in togas and gathering other students along the way as we excitedly planned a foray outside the dorm to recruit married students and spouses from their on-campus apartments. After succeeding in getting a few to join us, the fifteen-to-twenty of us went to Professor Tim Lull's home located a short walk away, by the perimeter of campus. The sun's setting rays illuminated us as we knocked on his door. Answering, this five-foot-four, learned man showed no reaction to our motley throng and simply asked, "What is this?"

"We've come to see the pope," someone said.

"Oh, I see. Wait one moment." He shut the door. This wasn't what we expected and we quietly shuffled our feet. *Should we go or stay? Was he upset with us?* As we tried to determine our next move, feeling far less toga-party-spirit, Dr. Lull emerged on the second floor balcony of his home, wearing his black academic robe and red hat and began to speak to us in Latin as he blessed us. We laughed joyously. He invited the party into his home where his wife was bringing out wine, beer, cheese, and crackers. It was a memorable night of hilarity. It makes me so glad to have been there, to have felt so alive, and to have been among those wonderful Christians.

Unconditional love and acceptance. I seldom experienced it in college. When I would hear people say that college was "the best years of your life," I thought that I had missed that train for sure. Now I was zipping along the fast track with the secure feeling that God was with me as I was learning how to be God's servant. Community in a congregation would be similar, I assumed: Christians enjoying each other's company and feeling blessed in their association. My experiment with seminary had started off marvelously.

Not so marvelous, however, was my relationship with Aaron as time passed. Now that I was immersed in a community where I was free to be myself, Pretend Margie was quickly disappearing. Feedback I got from professors, students, and mentors was that they admired my forthrightness. Male friends told me they liked my honesty. Forthright? Honest? Thus began a new level of self-awareness.

Tony, a second year student, and I would meet regularly for study time and he, in particular, broadened my view of myself. "Margie, you don't hide things about yourself. That's refreshing and not what I'm used to in women." I liked him. He was funny, using a clever sense of humor to put people at ease. His goatee beard and mustache helped to lengthen his round face, which suited his short, square build. I felt an unexpected attraction to him that led me to run, not walk, to see a professor for counseling. *How can I be engaged to Aaron and have feelings for Tony? What's going on with me?*

Through that counselor's guidance, I became aware of Pretend Margie for the first time. He also knocked me over my head with the obvious. "It sounds like you would like to be free to explore a relationship with Tony." Well, of course I did, but the counselor saying it out loud made that clear.

In early November I planted myself on the chair in the hallway of the dorm to call Aaron. With no phones in our rooms, I had no other choice. "I'm not sure about our relationship anymore, Aaron. I love you, but I realize how I've messed up. I messed us up."

The concern was apparent in his voice. "What could you have messed up? Tell me what's going on with you."

"Well, I did you and us a great disservice by not really being me. I know that now."

"I don't understand what you're talking about. When were you not you?"

Then I told him with a weepy thickened voice, so many things: how I hid my TV watching, that I liked to swear, that I wanted us to be able to have alcohol in our future home if I wanted and not be teetotalers as he had desired, that I had big issues with his parents and their resistance to my becoming a pastor. I tried to explain how the seminary community had awakened me. Students walked by from time to time and saw my tears as I talked to him.

"How can two months in a place change you so much?" Aaron was stunned.

Reality poured out of me, and I shouted, "I woke up! This is the real me, Aaron. I was lying to myself and you. I don't know what to do." Naturally, he was more than disquieted by my revelations. Another student walked by, overhearing Aaron's stunned response through the phone. There was no privacy for me, the worm who was hurting Aaron like this. But, I also knew that my butterfly wings were finally spreading wide. The conversation was freeing, even amidst my anguish. We agreed to meet in Oley over Thanksgiving break to decide what to do.

I did not take my friendship with Tony to the next step of dating. It wasn't right, although we did discuss my dilemma regarding Aaron as well as the spark we felt between us. Tony was funny and outwardly social in a very appealing way. He struggled as a student academically but had a style with people that told me he would be an approachable, caring pastor. I was able to observe him among our peers and could not help but compare his engaging manner against Aaron's more reserved, quiet nature. Tony was not as good-looking as Aaron. He was pudgy, whereas Aaron was lithe. Tony was my height. I enjoyed looking up to Aaron. I felt entirely comfortable with Tony and knew he accepted me, the real me. That was a fresh breeze in my life.

On Thanksgiving weekend Aaron met me at my childhood home and we went to the only private place in the house to talk, my bedroom. We lay on the bed together, sharing our new lives—his as a teacher in a city culture and mine as a newly self-aware woman. It was both awkward and effortless as words tumbled from both of us.

"I don't think it's right for us to stay engaged, Aaron. It's not genuine, not with the way things are."

"I hate to say it, but, I guess you're right, Margie. But we'll keep talking and writing. I want to know the new you. I love you."

"I love you, too."

"I want this to work out. I feel like a jerk for making you feel like you had to hide yourself. I'm too controlling."

"Not your fault. It's mostly me. I wanted you to love me, I guess, so I tried to fit what you wanted. I'm the one who's the jerk with too low a self-image to have been real."

We looked at each other and smiled sadly, both trying to take the blame. I gave him back the ring but we affirmed that we were still a couple. My mother marveled that we walked out of the house holding hands. We tenderly kissed goodbye.

Before the snow of Christmas, Aaron called me and officially broke it off. How could I blame him? It was the right thing to do for both of us. I followed up with a letter to that dear man, my first love, trying to adequately express my gratitude for our time together. I had loved him fiercely and had been raised up by his love for me.

January term back at seminary was "all Greek, all the time." It was a four-week immersion in New Testament Greek with three-hour classes and loads of work each night to learn the language. Having studied high school and college German, Greek came easily for me since the grammar is similar, so I found myself with free time that many of my classmates did not. Tony and I used that time to "date." Neither of us had much money to go places so the dates were mostly in my dorm room. He had a roommate but as Mary had taken the second semester off, I had the suite to myself. Tony and I used that privacy for making out, which was everything (And I mean everything.) but intercourse as we both maintained our virginity. My Goody Two-shoes ways were gone.

Did I feel guilty about it? No. Yet, I looked with judgment on another male student in my class who was engaged to be married and sexually active with his future wife. How could he be doing that and preparing to be a pastor? At that time I believed that intercourse was to be saved for marriage. That is what the church taught. Sex outside marriage was a "clear" sin. Tony and I did not cross that line. But still, I was conflicted about the muddied line of sexual righteousness in general.

~

Newness often intimidates. Mahatma Gandhi said, "Be the change that you wish to see in the world." As a female seminarian, I was in the position of being the change and took satisfaction in knowing I was pioneering a new path. I was part of changing the world. And even though it came out years after I became a pastor, Apple Incorporated's ad celebrating "the crazy ones" who think they can change the world—and so they do—always struck a chord with me because it's true.

I was not the only crazy one. Two women were ordained in my Lutheran denomination in 1970. In 1980, when I was ordained, I was among 63 women across the country added to the ranks of Lutheran pastors, contrasted with 353 men—15%. In 2008, 165 women were ordained; 168 men—50%. It remains similar to this day. The crazies have multiplied to normal status, one would think, but today I still receive comments such as, "You're the first woman preacher I have ever seen."

Lutheran pastors wear clerical collars and shirts, customarily black but available in other colors, with either an insertable plastic tab white collar in the front or a stiff white collar that wraps around the neck. They can be binding and uncomfortable, especially on hot days, but they identify me as a pastor so I put up with them as a necessary uniform, which is especially useful for making hospital calls: I can gain access to patient rooms and garner immediate respect from the medical personnel much more speedily than when I am in my street clothes.

As a new seminarian, I had been expected to work on Sundays at a Field Education parish to practice the basics of worship leadership and teaching. To identify myself as a seminarian, I was to wear a clerical collar. Now, almost fifty years after the advent of ordained women among the Lutherans, Episcopalians, and some other denominations, there is clergy garb made just for women, but in my seminary days, I found it was a man-only world of clothing. In my first month at seminary another female student, Anna, and I drove to the Lutheran church bookstore in Philadelphia that also sold clergy shirts and robes. All the incoming students, male and female, had been told to buy at least one clergy shirt to wear when leading worship at our assigned Sunday congregations.

My new friend and I were in good humor and excited about getting our blouses until we stood before the shelves on which the clergy shirts for men were arranged by size and color. "Where are the clergy blouses?" I asked a clerk nearby.

"Clergy blouses! Nobody makes those." He laughed so hard that his ample belly moved up and down while he appraised us. "The church may have voted for women pastors but we obviously aren't encouraging it, it seems."

Images of Gordon consigning me to hell flashed by. Anna saw it in my face and touched my arm before calmly responding, "We're students at the seminary—female students—and we need to buy clergy attire. This is all you have?"

He looked us up and down. I stood my normal five feet, seven inches and 122 pounds. Anna was five-ten and 170. "I'm frustrated as to what to do for you girls. You're not the first girls to come in here. I tell them all the same thing. You can measure your necks so you can buy a man's shirt close to your size." As he pointed at Anna's ample chest he continued, "But I don't know what you're gonna do about those. I don't know if the shirt that fits your neck will be big enough in the chest to accommodate 'em."

Anna placed her hands under her breasts pushing them up a bit. "They're nice though, huh?" He took a step back in shock. "I could see you looking at them, but I won't tell." With that, she gave him a playful little punch on the arm and laughed. "Oh come, on we won't bite ya."

I held my breath and witnessed her charming this man with her easy wit and joking manner. Our pudgy, befuddled clerk responded with kindness. He directed us to possible sizes among the packaged shirts neatly stacked and individually wrapped in plastic. I asked, "Uh, do you have any we can try on? These are all wrapped in plastic."

"Well, I do have a few display shirts that you might try in various sizes."

"How about a tape measure for our necks?"

He sighed. "The men always come in knowing their size and don't need measuring. We also don't have a fitting room. You'll have to use the restroom. We mostly sell books here." His bewilderment showed as he shook his head from side to side. Sighing again he said, "I'll go look for a tape measure."

As he walked away Anna called after him, "Can you bring the pink clergy blouses with you when you come back?" He turned and smiled, still captivated by Anna's good humor. She was a soothsayer; today clergy blouses do come in pink.

I left the store with one shirt, size fourteen-and-a-half neck, which was too loose but was the smallest they had. The shirttails hung to my thighs. It would have to do until I could figure out how to use my sewing skills to make a proper clergy blouse. By the time of my internship, two years later, I had sewn several. They were much more stylish, tailored with darts, puffy sleeves, and with tails the appropriate length. I even made two styles of clergy dresses. (Years later I made a black maternity clergy dress for myself, too.) Those who could not sew were stuck with the men's shirts for years or had to hire a seamstress. Today, for life in Florida, I make sleeveless clergy blouses.

Some adults in my Field Ed church were accepting of my presence as a legitimate student and others seemed aghast, heads shaking in a what-is-this-world-coming-to manner. Children, however, were happy, as kids are, to have me pay attention to them. For them, my collar made me represent someone who would simply love them. One Sunday I was with a group of kids in the fellowship hall after worship. They were waiting for permission to dive into the food laid out for the coffee hour, which was especially attractive that day because the bishop had preached at the worship service as a guest.

Seeing the ones who were trying to sneak a few cookies, I stopped the planned thievery with a smile. "You can't eat yet. We have to wait for the bishop."

Little Jamal looked up at me with his dark face, brown eyes sparkling. "Is it a boy pastor or a girl pastor?"

Well, what do you know? An out-of-the-mouths-of-babes moment. "The bishop is a man pastor," I responded, thrilled that the seed had been planted in that child that pastors came in both genders.

Later in my first parish as pastor, a boy of about age eight was absolutely stunned when he saw a male pastor who was visiting our church. He stopped in mid-stride, put his hands on his hips, staring. "Pastor Margie, you mean boys can be pastors, too?" What a difference a few decades can make.

Clothes for women pastors were but a minor adjustment compared to the shift that professors had to make with women on campus. For hundreds of years, seminary was a male bastion guiding the church. Women students' presence was a new challenge. Further, the male professors, who were the majority, (There were just two women on the faculty at my school.) had language issues. After years of teaching just men, it was obviously difficult for some of them to adjust to saying "he or she" when referring to pastors in lectures and conversations. They also needed to shift away from the term "clergy wives" and use the gender-neutral, "spouses." Usually, some brave or cocky person would correct them so that they soon learned to be more gender-inclusive in their language.

One professor who was very tall always seemed to be looking down women's shirts. We women would discuss it with laughter, not being able to decide if he actually was taking a peek or if it was his height (and reading glasses perched on his nose) that made it appear that he was enjoying the cleavage. It was fun to speculate about it and did not offend us.

Together, professors and students were breaking new ground in that first decade of women clergy and we all tried to ride the wave of change with grace and good humor. Truly, I received nothing but support and equal consideration from the men on the faculty and staff. They wanted women to succeed, championing us as a good development for the future of the church. It was another sign of grace in a Christian community on a campus that I adored.

~

Tony and I did not last, by my choice. I faced the sad reality that I could not see myself falling in love with him, ever, so I did a mercy killing of the splendid "us" we had been. At the end of my first year, I moved to Kalamazoo, Michigan, for my summer of Clinical Pastoral Education. CPE is a ten-week period of work in some sort of an institution as a student chaplain. Mine was a hospital. Six other students and I, under the supervision of the hospital chaplain, were forced to get raw and deep as we struggled with issues of illness, death, dying, and our own inadequacies. It was all part of learning to provide pastoral care.

CPE group sessions were not for the fainthearted. Our intense discussions of theology and pastoral visitation were challenging, but the riskiest moments were when we critiqued each other's "verbatims," which were written regurgitations (from memory) of conversations we had had with patients. Counseling and pastoral care techniques gleaned from textbooks were sterile compared to the reality of my daily assignments visiting patients. I saw cancer, breast reduction, disease, death, and a failed suicide attempt that left a man with a severely damaged face from the gunshot. It was a demanding but exciting challenge to learn how to be the presence of God in each hospital room. Often I would pray with them in what I thought was a helpful manner, while other times I left a bedside feeling inadequate and helpless.

I was feeling more content in my vocational choice but faced the reality of a future without a mate. I surely knew that female pastors were not the number one choice in the dating landscape. I was at a bar one night with a female acquaintance from the hospital and was approached by an intriguing man. He bought me a drink, and we talked easily. Then he asked me what I did for a living. Within moments I was drinking alone.

One night when I was the on-call chaplain for the Emergency Room I had a meltdown. I never could have anticipated it. I was buzzed on my pager to attend to the situation of a thirteen-year-old boy brought in following a dirt bike crash. So I went to the private waiting room to be with his mother while we awaited word of his condition. Her placement into a private waiting area was not a good sign. I didn't expect a positive outcome but was nevertheless pleased with how I handled the situation pastorally. I engaged her in conversation about her son, learning about his personality and pursuits. He sounded like a bright, eager-to-please boy.

My verbatim to my CPE group later included the following: ...his mother lamented, "I wasn't keen on his getting that bike. I was worried about something like this happening and now it has! It's my fault." Her body shuddered.

I quietly let her weep and finally interjected, "You feel it's your fault, yes, but would he say it's your fault?"

"Uh, no, he loved that bike and was the happiest kid when he could ride it on the trails around our house."

"He was happy with that bike." (To echo back what a person says was an active listening technique I had learned. It encourages the other to say more.)

"Yes, very much so. He told us how much he loved us for trusting him with the responsibility."

"A teenage boy expressing love to his parents. Amazing kid. So this was clearly an accident, then."

"Yes, it was. No one's fault. No one's."

Her husband soon arrived and I watched as she stood up and launched herself into his arms, sobbing. As he held her I explained to him what we knew about his son. Within moments a doctor came in and knelt before them as they sat at the couch. He reviewed the trauma to their boy's head in the crash. "We have done everything in our power to help your son, but his injuries were too extensive. I am sorry to tell you that your son has died." I sat in a chair opposite and observed them fall into each other as their lives changed forever. They asked a few questions of the doctor and I left the room to give them time alone. After helping them contact a local funeral home I prayed with them and other family members who had arrived. They all thanked me for my time.

I strode from the hospital, tortured for them, but glad for me that I had had such an experience to take to my CPE group for discussion. Oddly, I felt lucky. Then as I drove to my apartment I began to cry. I didn't know why I was crying. The loss of that young life? I cried and cried, and cried some more, trying to see the road and really needing to blow my nose. (I am a snotty weeper.)

I parked the car, crying. I entered the apartment, crying. I changed my clothes, crying. I tried to stop. *Maybe some TV.* I cried some more. Food was impossible to consume because I couldn't stop the tears. How much time went by? Two hours. Maybe more. I began to worry. *What's wrong with me?* Finally, I called Chaplain Davis, my CPE supervisor. He patiently listened as I tried to explain what was going on between my sobs. Even though it was not a drug-induced freak-out, I guess he "talked me down." As I listened to his voice of reason and his assurance that he would help me figure it out the next day, I was soothed from sobs to sniffles, and finally my sanity returned. I hung up the phone, ate some yogurt and watched Johnny Carson. The boy was still dead.

So what had happened? Mercifully, Chaplain Davis didn't bring my sob experience to the entire group for analysis, only how I had handled it in the ER through my verbatim. We met privately to unpack the unexpected emotional jag. He threw out some theories. It could have been 1) unresolved grief over the loss of Aaron, 2) my facing death for the first time, 3) who the hell knew? I went with door number one since it made the most sense. It was seven months from that breakup, Tony was out of my life, and I had recently passed the June date that was to have been my wedding day. These had been "deaths" that I had not grieved. Perhaps my strong, adventurous, competitive armor had a proverbial chink, revealing the little girl in me who feels all alone, still swaying on her childhood swing, feeling unloved.

After that very maturing summer chaplaincy, my second-year

classmates and I returned to campus abuzz with our tales of CPE, pleased to see the growth we had experienced from the intense reality of feelings—our own and those of the people to whom we had ministered. *Maybe I can actually be a pastor.* I fell back into a routine of classes (Corinthians, Reformation History, Theology, Preaching) and Sunday duties at my new Field Education congregation. I was very happy to be back.

The senior students who had returned from year-long internships were an interesting and fun group to get to know and I bantered with them in the dining hall while serving their tables. One evening I approached a table with a hot plate of vegetables and overheard laughter over a gay joke told by one of the students who himself was gay. This I found remarkable: both the joke-teller and the presence of gay people on campus. It was "known" that homosexual students were on campus but seldom discussed since they had to keep their sexuality a secret.

Around that time, I had become friends with a man named Ben. He was tall and slender, dark-haired, a senior, and a deeply spiritual man with a great passion for urban ministry. Yet, he was cautious and not one to easily share himself. I realized why when he told me that he lived two lives—the "acceptable seminary student" life and the "closeted gay" life. Flattered by his trust in me and intrigued, I learned valuable walk-a-mile-in-his-shoes lessons by speaking with him.

Ben told me of a subculture my small-town mind could not have imagined. For example, one night stands were standard. "How can you have sex with someone you just met?" I asked in shock. His answer was that (beyond wanting the sexual release) in order to meet someone who might become a life partner, sex came first in gay culture, relationship second.

"That's so opposite of the heterosexual standard of courtship. How come?"

"Because we can't openly date, Margie. Think about it. How am I gonna find someone other than the only way it is for us homos to get to get to know each other?"

"Oh, I hate that word. Don't you?" Ben shrugged his shoulders. "But what about the church's teaching that homosexuality is wrong?"

"Wrong to the men who wrote the law calling it an abomination in Leviticus, maybe, but they also said you should stone to death a child who curses his parents and said it was okay to sell your daughters into slavery. We're not Biblical literalists, you know that."

"Jesus never did have a thing to say about it, did he?"

"Nope, but he did talk about love. The greatest commandment is to love God; love others. Without that word from Christ, I might as well be dead." I could not imagine the anguish behind that statement.

Was I appalled? By what seemed to be casual sex for my friend? Absolutely. Some of the mental images made me bug-eyed. But I was more filled with compassion that Ben had to hide who he was. I was not the only one with a pretend alter ego it seemed. He told me, "I knew I was different from about five years old. I just didn't have a label for it. When I realized as a teen I was a homosexual, I wanted to die. I thought about suicide. I prayed that I would change, but of course, I didn't."

"So, now you have to keep this secret in order to be ordained?"

"Not just for ordination, but from many family members and certain friends."

Ben was a gifted preacher and worship leader, a fine person with this one big "dark spot" in the eyes of the Church. The Church of that time (the standard is to capitalize the word when referring to the church at large) would not accept a gay pastor—it was sin—so my friend kept his secret in order to follow his heart, and God's call, to become a pastor. I kept his secret as well.

Through Ben, I became friends with another senior. Luke lived down the hall from me in the dorm. This sandy-haired, rail thin, coffee-and-pastry lover had a staccato laugh that resonated in whatever space he occupied. His enthusiasm, sense of humor and ability to point out some bizarre happening on campus with wide-eyed, little-boy astonishment and mirth made him a people magnet. You could not dislike Luke. His stops at my door on the way to his room became more frequent and he regaled me with stories from his internship, slapping his knee and laughing each time. With an ability to see the humor in some of the quirkier people in his Long Island internship parish, he charmed me by putting a positive spin on even less-than-loving Christians. This man could not wait to get into a parish as a pastor so he could share his love of worship liturgy done right, organ music, and helping people. I greatly admired his devotion and learned practical ministry skills from his example and stories. What fun he was.

He liked me too, and we happily became a couple. I was lonely no more.

Debbie Boone's one-hit wonder, *You Light Up My Life,* was popular in early 1978 and it became our song. We sang along to it. We danced to it at campus dances, two skinny, happy, laughing people observed by our fellow students, who took pleasure in seeing our love develop. The song defined the way we felt about each other. Whenever we went off campus for a date, he would drive his small car while often keeping his right hand on my left knee. Unlike Mr. Barker in the plane, this was an authentic sign of affection, inconsequential in appearance, but marking his attachment to me. He did light up my life.

After the Christmas snows and brief visits with our families between semesters, we each returned to campus to pursue important life advancements—my internship location and his first job/call to parish ministry. We hoped they could be geographically close to each other. Therefore, I pursued internships in northeast Pennsylvania where he would most likely be ordained and serve his first congregation. It was all going to work out. I projected myself forward in time a few years and saw us married, both serving as pastors in congregations near each other or perhaps serving one congregation as co-pastors. Finding parishes close by was not easy, but with the increasing numbers of men and women together on seminary campuses, students were naturally falling in love and marrying. It was new territory for the bishops who assisted in finding locations for such couples, but I was hopeful. Surely the Holy Spirit could lead even clergy couples to just the right placements for each.

One evening, Luke drove us into the city where his favorite organist was performing. He talked the same, laughed the same, looked the same. However, he didn't place his hand on my knee. Luke was not the same. *Oh, he's just worried that we won't make it to the concert in time. He's concentrating on the road. Everything's fine. No worries, Marjorie. He loves you.* On our next car trip, sans hand on knee once again, I knew it down to my toes that his feelings toward me had shifted. I didn't know why and didn't ask him about it. I didn't want to face his answer.

Luke and I continued to see each other until the end of the semester. His laughter and reassuring presence kept me from dwelling on my doubts for our future. "You'll do a great job, Margie. Just wait until your internship. That'll make the difference for you. Look how skilled you are, and smart, and courageous. You're dating me aren't you? That takes bravery to the nth degree," he laughed and pulled me close. *Everything is fine.* I willed myself to believe it.

Chafing at the need to finish his last semester of academics, especially with a demanding and unsympathetic professor who required translations of the New Testament book of Corinthians directly from the Greek, Luke was impatient and more caffeined up than usual. He noticeably calmed down after he breezed through the interview process with a congregation that led to his receiving a call to a small church in a northeast Pennsylvania town.

I had a bead on an internship not far away from his parish-to-be that I thought pleased us both. Two of my classmates, who were engaged, were worried about my interest, however. Beth had already secured her internship and Bobby wanted the position at the site I was interested in so he could be near her. I told Luke about the dilemma one day while we studied together in his dorm room.

"I could possibly go to Jamestown, New York, but why shouldn't I get that internship near Scranton? With Pastor Papada, my former home pastor? He'd be my supervisor. You know how much he meant to me."

"Yeah, but Bobby and Beth oughta be together. They're gonna get married." Luke sipped his coffee, unaware of how his words had just reached out and bitten me.

"I know. I know. But what about us?"

"We're not engaged."

"But we're a couple and I want to be able to see you. If I go to Jamestown we'd be apart so long. It's all the way over near Lake Erie, not a short trip to see you." I slid across the couch to where he was sitting and kissed his cheek for emphasis.

"There's phones, ya know. It's only a year." He laughed in his engaging manner but didn't put this arm around me. "Which site excites you more, Wilkes Barre or Jamestown?" Typical Luke, getting to the professional heart of it for me. It was the right question.

I'd never lived out of the state other than that brief summer in Michigan...Maybe my former pastor wouldn't be the best supervisor for me...Jamestown is bigger, and the congregation has a thriving ministry...It's got an after-school program and outreach to the poor... Could be a great learning experience. Might be a better for me.

And so, I took a chance on Jamestown rather than going with what was safe and known—rather than choosing Luke. He was happy for me, perhaps relieved. His hand never did return to my knee.

It was replaced instead by a large elephant who looked at me with a doleful smile. She said, "Don't you think you two should talk about me? You know what the problem is even if he doesn't. You complicate things too much. He loves you but can't face the reality of being married to a pastor and what that will mean for his future calls to congregations. Don't you think? You're a distraction, not part of the plan. I think he's afraid of you being in his future."

That elephant was heavily on me when I attended Luke's ordination. He introduced me to his family as his sweetheart, but it seemed flat. A month later it was I who was heavy as I tearfully sank to the floor, into the rough folds of the elephant's skin, and let her wrap her trunk around me. Luke had phoned and ended our relationship. "You should have listened to me. I told you so," said my pachyderm friend.

"I know. I know."

She hugged me close and whispered, "Alone again."

The Growing Wall

Alone. That's how I felt post Cinder Block Room without the God who had been my companion. God and I always journeyed together, our little car purring along, God's hand on my knee. I was secure in that love. God was devoted to me, my guide and rock. The Old Testament calls it *"hesed."* The translation of this Hebrew word is steadfast love, ever-faithful, and constantly-pursuing. That image had sustained me ever since I had learned of it in Old Testament class and it had always given me hope for my future. *Could it still?* I wondered as I continued to deconstruct my life to understand each cinder block. My journals give me a timeline that showed a decreasing connection with a God entity. In the 1990s, my journal entries were often letters to God, seeking a word of advice and the proverbial shelter from the storm. I would often use the technique of free flow writing as if God were answering me through my own pen. I felt that God spoke to me through his/her letters in those journals, often amazing me with insights as I lamented my husband's depression in that decade.

I also wrote about the troubles we were having with our daughter, Lynn, in the harrows of teenage agony at that time. No longer the malleable, newly adopted eight-year-old who had first moved in with us in 1987, reaching adolescence had brought to light the deep wounds she had. Adoption can be challenging for any child, but for Lynn, it was doubly so. Not only did she feel rejection from her birth parents, but also from the first couple who had adopted her and with whom she had lived from age two to eight. They had abandoned her, giving her back to the state.

Lynn, unknowingly, worked hard to get us to kick her out too. "My self-esteem was in the toilet, Mom," she'll say today. "I thought I didn't deserve any good thing." She spent her high school years as an angry spitting "push me-pull you," never knowing which direction to go in relationships, studies, or family issues. It was a very lonely walk for us as parents. Lonelier for her.

My July 27, 1994, journal entry: (Lynn was a few weeks shy of sixteen years old.)

> *Lord, I don't know what to do about Lynn. She's talking suicide again. I know magic is not going to change anything, but...She's her own worst enemy and makes her life miserable. Things won't change until she does and I'm powerless to do anything. I hate the situation, the tenseness, the feeling of*

> *discomfort in my own house. I wind up then hating her as a result and don't like that about myself. Help me. Help her. It's the situation I hate, not her.*
>
> *God replied: Margie, I love you. I love Lynn too and I want to help her. I will help her. The struggles will continue so be strong. Persevere, and know that I am with you. Put this in my hands and let go of your need to control. Do what you can and then let go. I'll be there no matter what. Love, God.*

God had obviously been alive and real to me even in a bleak time.

That surety began to shift, however. Three years later, October 6, 1997, I journaled about a lovely walk on an 80° Pennsylvania fall day.

> *As I watched the trees rustle in the calming breeze and enjoyed the sounds of nature in my walk, I wondered that life/work/commitments get in the way of living. There is such beauty around and I am blind to it. My life is passing on quickly and I feel I am missing a lot. But what?... God. I am missing God. I do and say the right stuff at church and obviously pass it on well, very well, but I miss a daily walk with God. It is too remote, that walk. I am on a path and Jesus is like a marionette that*

pops in from time to time—or is it vice versa? I pop in when it is convenient or I need help. Otherwise, I dangle above, alone.

God's loving hand was no longer on my knee. My elephant looked at me and said, "We've been here before, Margie. Don't you think you should talk to someone about this?" I didn't… those cinder blocks.

On many summer evenings when I was young, my father would be on the front porch. His presence there was a lure for me to leave the TV to go and sit with him. It was a special time for me to be, not one of four children, but one child. We talked or played games like sinking each other's battleships on our paper grids. I would watch him as he conversed with those strolling by. They would call him Herbie, a name he never liked but tolerated gracefully. We would also watch traffic. The old guy in the red two-seater convertible sports car wearing an Irish tweed hat was one of my favorites. The street was a mere ten feet from our porch steps, and from that view, we could see the spot where I had gotten hit by that car a few years before.

"Look at the lovebirds!" Dad said, his eyes crinkling as he smiled. He pointed to a car approaching, driven by a young man, his girlfriend sitting in the middle of the front bench seat, right next to him.

"Lovebirds? What's that, Daddy?" I asked as I went to sit in his lap.

"A young couple who are so much in love that they like to sit close when they're in the car."

"Did you and Mommy sit that way?"

"Yup, we sure did."

"Why don't you sit that way anymore?"

"Why? Because one of you kids is usually sitting there, that's why!" He tweaked my cheek and held me close.

"Do you think I'll get to be a lovebird someday?"

"Well, you're sitting close to me right now, aren't you? So I guess that makes us lovebirds!"

"Oh, Daddy!" I playfully hit his arm, content to be loved in that moment. The lure of the front porch was love.

A sermon illustration I once used described a middle-aged couple traveling by car. The wife said, "Honey, remember when we used to drive somewhere and I'd sit right next to you, snuggled up?" She sighed and continued, "Why don't we do that anymore?"

His response was, "Well, dear, I haven't moved."

In that sermon, I was trying to illustrate how we can drift from God. So when I "lost" God, did God leave me, or was I the one who had slid away from God? Even more vexing was this possibility: that I had been in a driverless car of faith, lured there by a love that didn't exist. I had become a passenger and was on the proverbial Sunday drive when the car rounded a corner and suddenly crashed through a guardrail, down a cliff, to the rocks below. No, no, this cannot be! A God of love, calling me into a relationship and then abandoning me? I was on a quest, lured still by love.

Lose my relationship with God? I once had thought it impossible. I had believed that I was not really as alone as I sometimes felt. God knew me. I was going to share that love with others. God was leading me, of that I had no doubt. I now know, that the Cinder Block Room began to be mortared together in 1978, when I began my internship at Immanuel Lutheran Church, Jamestown, New York. Arriving in Jamestown, I was happy to be immersed in full-time congregational ministry and to be learning how much of parish ministry is relational. A pastor needs to get to know the people. I did this through home visits, hospital calls, committee meetings, Sunday school, and social events. At suppers, I was introduced to *korv,* a Swedish sausage. Many of the people of the parish shared in the Scandinavian sternness of their heritage but were kind and devoted to God's work. They wanted to become their best for God. Overall, I liked them.

I also liked that they wanted me to succeed. As I struggled to preach relevant sermons, they looked at me eagerly, willing me along with their focus and attention. I found teaching adults very intimidating, but I was bolstered by the feedback of the people who were genuinely engaged and edified by the discussions I led. I did feel competitive with the legacy of the two interns who had preceded me, as my old scorekeeper voice told me I didn't preach as well as Marie nor did I lead the youth ministry with the creativity of Bill. Bob, my pastor supervisor, a young pastor of thirty-six, encouraged me to find my own identity and so I did, in teaching the teenage Sunday school class. There, the kids were glad that I tossed the stilted curriculum out the door and replaced it with topical discussions each week. Worship leadership also went well, particularly because I could sing the worship leader parts, which Bob did not do. I was having fun. It was an energizing place to be learning.

From my first week, I had been open with Bob about my vacillation about actually becoming a pastor. Despite two years of seminary, I was still dubious about taking on that public role. When Bob and I met for my six-month evaluation I told him of a remarkable insight. "What's that, Margie?" he asked me in his soft South Carolina drawl.

"I've realized that I want to be ordained!"

"Wow, big news! What happened to convince you?"

"Not sure. I just know that the other night as I was nodding off to sleep, I just felt it. It was as if my outside self, the one that watches me live my life, said, 'You can do this, you know. You have what it takes and can be good at it.' "

Bob beamed at me. "You *are* good at it. Of the interns I've supervised, you've been doing the best. You're appealing in your relationships, authentic in style, and have an earnestness that people appreciate. I'm glad you've had this realization. Makes going into the second half of your year here very positive. Now, let's talk about your goals."

Goals? Professionally, I was a sponge and learning all I could. Personally, I'd been trying to do things socially, other than church events, hoping to make at least one friend. I was lonely. Jamestown was a small city (one of the features that drew me there), but there were few things for a single person to do, besides frequent bars and clubs. I don't think me doing *that* would have looked good to parish members. And usually when there was something I was interested in doing, such as attending a concert or a lecture, it fell on an evening I had to work. As an intern, I worked three to four nights a week—meetings, classes, or counseling appointments—just as most pastors do. As my internship progressed, I missed the camaraderie of seminary. I missed Luke.

People's reactions to me as a female intern pastor were at times hard to bear. For example, going bra-less is eminently comfortable, has never been a big deal to me, and is usually not noticeable to others. (That is a wonderful perk of being small-busted and happily, I had learned to really like that part of my anatomy.) Once, I bra-lessly helped the youth group with a car wash. On the day of that car wash, the temperature had dropped unexpectedly and "ping-ping" resulted—my self-chosen slang for erect nipples. Boy did I hear about it later. How inappropriate I was, how daring and un-pastor-like it had been. "The state of my underwear is no one's concern but mine!" I lamented to Bob.

"It is if it gets in the way of your pastoral image, Margie. And, if it gets in the way of someone hearing the gospel from you."

Reluctantly, I had to agree and have carefully hidden any public bra-lessness with over-shirts and shawls ever since. I never knew when someone from the church might be around the corner. The "real" me would be bra-less all the time as I just hate wearing them. Pretend Margie had to be resurrected to help me hide things about myself in order to be an effective pastor. I was now in a fishbowl in which people observed and judged what I did, said, and looked like.

Some folks had strong ideas about women clergy. Unusual opinions. Unexpected opinions. On one sunny fall afternoon I was at the home of Janette, a recently retired member of the congregation with whom I was working in planning a church fellowship dinner. We sat on the steps of her back porch sipping lemonade, inhaling the scent of the roses blooming in her garden, and enjoying the view of the maple tree above it, just starting to change color. Conversation flowed as Janette told me of her work as an executive secretary and how she was using those organizational skills at the church.

"How'd you get along with your bosses through the years?" I asked.

"I liked them all. Good men. I was blessed by that because some bosses can be awful."

"That's true. My mom had one like that, but I wonder if that's the case with women bosses? You've always worked for men?"

"Oh yes. I can't imagine working for a woman."

"Why's that?" I wondered.

"It would've felt strange."

"Do women pastors seem strange to you, too?"

"A bit. Yeah. It's okay if women want to be pastors. Marie did a good job, you're doing a good job. It's okay as long as you don't take jobs away from the men. They have to support their families."

I had heard this before. One of my pastor supervisors at seminary, a man only six years older than I was, had once said the same thing, no matter that women need to support their families, too...yet, ironically, women have not taken parish jobs away from men. We have a clergy shortage in my denomination. Without women, it would be much more severe. In that first decade of women being allowed to become pastors I had learned that I had a daunting hill to climb.

The cinder block mason kept building. Sexism hit again in one of my visits with Fred, a retiree from the congregation. He was easygoing, naughty in a charming way, and he made me feel valued by expressing his appreciation of my visits and by his positive words overall about my ministry at the congregation. I treasured the fact that he treated me like a normal person, freely swearing if he wanted to and telling me mildly off-color jokes. We would sit in his family room enjoying Bloody Marys together. One afternoon after we had discussed some church-related things he asked, "How are ya liking your internship so far?"

"Fred, I came here not sure I could be a pastor, but these months of doing pastor things has sealed the deal for me. I'm gonna do this."

"Well, good for you." Then he leaned forward to get closer to me. "You know, Margie, I think you would make a better wife than a pastor." I just about spit out my drink!

"Man, why would you say that?...Wow, wow, wow. Why can't I do both?"

"Why would you want to? You can be like Betty here and

stay home to raise the kids and let your husband take care of you." Betty entered the room and I saw her wince. He was just being his old fart self. It was a generational thing, I knew, but I was flabbergasted and hurt that he was the deliverer of such antiquated views.

His wife later apologized for him. "He was trying to give you a compliment because he likes you so much."

"I guess so, but it stunned me." I knew he'd hit me in a weak spot, the one that continued to make me think that ordination meant kissing the possibility of a husband goodbye. However, I hoped I could prove Fred wrong. In true women's lib-speak I wanted to have it all.

It had been a valuable foundational year for me. Preaching, worship leadership, teaching, setting a vision for outreach and service, being invited into people's lives at the important times of birth, illness and death—such were the points of parish ministry during which I had found passion in Jamestown. Certainly, that year also showed me the challenges I was going to face, but I expected that things would be different when I was a pastor and could set my own course. Yeah, naïve, I know.

Maybe, I should have listened to the Monty Python actors in my subconscious who were urging me repeatedly to run away. I wonder who I'd be now if I had? A happier person, or a purposeless one?

Internship enabled me to establish a relationship with the bishop of that area. Rewinding back for a moment, after a very happy and fulfilling fourth year at seminary, Bishop Ed Perry had offered to interview me for a dual call to serve as part-time solo pastor at Ascension Lutheran Church in Rome, New York, and also as a part-time associate pastor at Our Saviour Lutheran Church in Utica, fifteen miles away. I was to live in Rome and make the commute to Our Saviour on the days I was scheduled to work there. The interviews went well. I just had to talk myself into liking cold weather and the deep snow of the area's winters. I was super excited to begin my work as The Reverend Marjorie Weiss. Pastor Weiss—I liked the sound of it.

Rome was a small city that Bishop Perry had promised me would offer social opportunities for a twenty-six-year-old single woman. I accepted the offer and began my ministry in July 1980, getting to know members of both congregations during backyard picnics, boat rides, and home visits. I liked the newness. I was thriving on people. It was going to be great.

Ten months later I found myself pacing in my small office at Ascension, occasionally looking out at the backyard, seeing the grass that had grown to an extraordinary height, not yet mown by any volunteers. Who knew that as a pastor I would have to be concerned about mowing grass and bugging the volunteers to get it done? I stopped to watch the setting sun as I talked myself into toughness. Parish ministry was hard. I liked it. In fact, I loved so much of it—weekly preaching, being with people, helping people, and regular contact with children and teenagers. I was frustrated with myself for having any negative feelings. Wasn't I living my dream? What was wrong? I continued to pace, repeating in my mind the list of issues that had me feeling so unsettled.

For one, Eva, a new person to the Rome congregation—little Ascension, with about forty people at worship each week, did not get many new people—had told me that as she waited at the front door for her husband to pick her up each Sunday following worship, no one had spoken to her. Not once. At the time, she had already been worshipping with us for weeks. I wondered why she had even returned. The Ascensionites thought themselves very friendly and when I told a few about Eva they said it was *her* fault for not talking to *them*. Wow. Who were the hosts and who the guests? I never was successful in guiding them to see that.

Next, Catherine, a twenty-year member at Ascension reprimanded me in front of others, at the beginning of a Bible study, for not praying first. I liked to pray at the end to bring to God some of the issues from our discussions, and I felt Catherine had deliberately humiliated me. Was it because she felt I was a youngster whom she could tell what to do? Or was she one of the women who, statistics at that time showed, had more difficulty adjusting to a woman pastor than did men?

Then there was Don, a middle-aged father of three, always friendly to me and a leader in the church, who never once called me anything. Not Pastor, not Margie or Marjorie, not Ms. Weiss. Nothing. Heck, from him I even would have accepted Marge, which I dislike, just to have had him acknowledge me by name. It was amusing but also annoying. (Ironically, after Dave and I got married he began to call me Mrs. Derr, which

I told him was not accurate since my name remained Weiss. He went back to "Hey, you.")

Then there was Edgar, an elderly man who lived at a local nursing home, but was mobile enough to attend worship, and so volunteers would provide transportation for him each week. What a sweet, almost childlike person he was. I'd visit him at the home once a month, which always delighted both of us. He introduced me to his girlfriend at the home, Mary, who had dyed black hair and a suspicious demeanor. I could tell it would take me awhile to win her over, but I lost that opportunity. One day, she got upset with Edgar and me when I mentioned the pancake breakfast the church had had the Sunday before. "How could you go to that breakfast and not tell me? I thought you were going to church, not breakfast!" Her eyes blazed. She was irrational, of course, but Edgar stopped coming to church rather than lose Mary due to her jealousy. After that, he also no longer welcomed my visits to his nursing home. This innocent blunder crushed my youthful, inexperienced heart. People issues in the parish were certainly proving to be more of a challenge than I had expected.

The senior pastor in Utica and I got on well, but he had been highly critical of my novice preaching style, which added more tension to my already tension-filled weekly writing task. Additionally, a critique I received from both congregations was: "Pastor Weiss needs to smile more!" Apart from wondering if a male pastor would ever hear the same thing—You gotta smile more, Sonny—I didn't smile as much as I "should" because I felt exposed when I showed my teeth. Rationally, I knew I was not unattractive, but tell that to the child within who still heard the kids say, "Weiss has such funny teeth." I tried to do better in the smile department.

In contrast to Ascension, Our Saviour was a larger church with more diversity. I worked at Our Saviour two days a week, enjoying the activities and faster pace. Happily, I was able to draw a group of twenty folks to join a weekly Bible survey course. That was a major achievement since it required a two-year commitment. Together during these classes we chewed over the readings and Bible texts, and came to understand how comprehensive the love of God was. I adored the class and the people. The topics stretched us, especially those in the Old Testament where God often seemed more like a terrorist slaying enemies than a loving parent. We looked for and found the thread of love in those passages and saw that the "killer God" came from the writer's bias and the historical context in which it was written. When working with metaphors and theological God language, it is a challenge to get faith to its simplest form. But interpreting the Bible non-literally was wonderfully freeing for the class, leading to insights on weighty matters such as: how can we live purposefully as the prophet Micah had guided? "What does God require of you?" he had written, "To do justice, love kindness, and walk humbly with God."

Despite that outstanding class in which I flourished as a teacher, I was unable to be immersed in the life of that congregation. I worshipped with them just once a month and began to feel like the guest pastor on those Sundays, there to preach, but never quite part of the community. People who were not part of the class barely knew me. During the week I often would visit shut-ins, but some of them only wanted my colleague, the male pastor. Yes, they openly asked for him only. I understood. Change is hard. I knew that.

Just as in internship, I missed my friends. Pre-internet, Facebook, and smart phones, staying in touch required the intentionality of writing letters or of making long distance phone calls, the cost of which was prohibitive. Despite Bishop Perry's marketing, Rome was *not* the thriving spot for singles he had described. I had plenty of solitude that I used to knit, read, bake, and watch television. Solitude is nourishing. Loneliness is not. Having a sense of community in a congregation and a place to belong were the things that had led me into ministry, but they were not to be mine, easily, at either congregation. I was learning that you are not "one of the guys" when you are the pastor. On internship I had been more like the beloved pet and was taken care of by a number of older surrogate parents. I had not foreseen the depth of isolation that I would experience as a full-time pastor.

Nevertheless, I maintained my usual optimistic outlook on life. The future had always held promise for me. My unique role as one of only two female pastors in Rome certainly got me noticed. I enjoyed shaking things up by embodying this new journey since it fed my adventurous spirit. On more than one occasion, I saw people rubberneck as they passed me on the street, at the mall, or in a hospital when I appeared publicly in my clerical collar. At that point in my life, I liked the attention and it made me smile.

Ruth Snyder was a Lutheran pastor in nearby Verona, New York. We'd been in seminary one year together, so had a shared history and would lunch together from time to time for support. I was glad for her friendship. At one point, three local Lutheran Church-Missouri Synod denomination pastors asked to meet with us. They wanted to discuss what it was like for us as women clergy. We were impressed that men from such a conservative Lutheran denomination were open to hearing our stories. (Missouri Synod Lutherans interpret the Bible more literally and do not ordain women or allow women in any leadership roles to this day. They are similar to fundamentalist Christians in many respects.)

On the appointed day, Ruth and I deliberately decided to wear our collars so as to be a visual billboard for the men. Five foot, three inch tall Ruth had two-foot-long, straight, blond hair, parted in the middle. She wore slacks and a light blue clerical shirt and pants since she disliked skirts. My brown hair was cropped short and I wore a gray shirt and collar with a skirt as I never wore slacks with clerics. In our late twenties at the time, we both embodied femininity and youthful good cheer. The Missouri Synod guys, all middle-aged, wore their clergy attire as well, all black, which is typical for that denomination. We must have been quite a sight, those three pitted against us two, which is what it turned out to be—a verbal match. What we had been told would be a "learning exchange between our two denominations" began with one of the MS pastors actually asking, "Do you ever preach the Gospel or just this feminist nonsense?"

Ruth's eyes flared, so I put my hand on her arm to indicate that I'd answer. "Of course, we do, that's the task of a pastor, to share the good news of Jesus' love, just as you do. Feminism is not an agenda item for us..."

Ruth interjected, "But we are in favor of the full inclusion of women in the life and leadership of the church."

The time we spent with them was not pleasant. Being grilled and vetted for positions for which we had already been qualified, as well as being called to defend the "errors" of our denomination, was demeaning. Nevertheless, we both felt we had handled ourselves well.

That meeting had done little to establish any true collegiality between me and the Missouri Synod pastor, just up the road from Ascension. A few months later, there was to be a wedding at a Missouri Synod congregation. The bride was a member there, the groom, a member of my congregation. Their families wanted me to participate as a pastor in the wedding, in partnership with the MS pastor who had been one of the above grillers. The MS congregational leadership denied their request, responding, "It's not proper for a female pastor to be in our chancel." (The chancel is the space around the altar of a church for the clergy, sometimes enclosed by a railing.) Hence, I did not get to co-officiate and instead sat in the pew with the others guests. When the pastor greeted me later that day, I told him that I looked to the day when such petty things did not divide us as Lutherans. "Ah, but it is not petty," was his reply. It was a no-win situation.

In a beautifully ironic moment soon after that wedding,

I was asked to preach for a joint Thanksgiving Eve service of Protestants and Catholics at the Roman Catholic Church in Rome. How fascinating. Roman Catholics continue to ordain only men, but that evening in 1981 there was no question of my being in the chancel. In fact, I was surprised and delighted when after the service their priest told me with obvious excitement, "You've just made history!" The Missouri Synod Lutherans, closer to me in doctrine had shunned me, but the Catholics were grace-filled and welcoming.

(Fast forward to 2004 when I again preached at a Catholic Church, this time in Wellington, Florida, at the joint Protestant-Catholic Thanksgiving Eve service. The topic, of course, was being thankful for blessings and how to share that with others. I recall using a fair amount of humorous stories which led to laughter in the pews. When I concluded, much to my surprise, the congregation applauded, a first for me, as it is not a typical, or often acceptable response to a sermon at Lutheran worship. I sat down at my assigned seat next to the Catholic priest and asked, "Do they applaud for you?" He quietly replied, "Never." Obviously, women have the abilities to be pastors and priests. I still await the full inclusion of woman as priests in the Catholic Church. How about it, Pope Francis?)

No matter. I savored being a maverick back then. One afternoon I walked into the hospital at the local air base and waited to find out the room number for the airman patient from the congregation I was sent to visit. The young lieutenant on duty saw my black clergy blouse and collar and blurted out as he rushed by, "I'll be right with you, Father." *Did he just call me Father?* When he returned he had obviously realized that that title didn't quite seem to fit my skirt and lipstick so he sheepishly asked, "What do I call you?"

"Pastor is appropriate."

"Sorry, Father…ma'am, er, Pastor. Oh sorry, again." His face reddened.

He was a dyed-in-the-wool Catholic if I ever saw one. "So, did you attend Catholic school?" I asked as he escorted me to the room.

"Yes, ma'am. Uh, Pastor. You can tell, huh?"

"The 'Father' title kinda gives it away."

"It does creep me out to see you dressed that way. My priest was tough on me. So were the nuns."

"Try worshipping with us at my church." I handed him my card. "You might like a kinder perspective." Did he come? Sadly, no.

Throughout the years I have indeed been called Father on several other occasions. It's always amusing for me to see the puzzlement on people's faces when they use the term and then look at the skirt and legs and feminine form. My collar still causes astonishment and, I have concluded, will do so until I die.

In 1993, twenty years after the lieutenant called me Father, I entered a hospital elevator wearing a black clergy blouse, black skirt, and a fuchsia blazer—always an attractive combination. The smartly dressed businesswoman already in the elevator looked me up and down. I was accustomed to being stared at by people when I was in my clergy garb but any of that kind of attention had long ago lost its glamour. (I eventually began to take the plastic tab out when not doing an official pastoral duty since I was tired of not appearing normal and being stared at by strangers.) This woman went beyond staring, however. "What *are* you?" she said with force.

"A human being, last I looked." I laughed. She did not smile. I quickly followed up.

"I'm a Lutheran pastor."

"Well, how long have they been doing that?"

"Ordaining women?"

"Yes."

"Thirty years or so in my denomination."

"Well, you're my first lady pastor. It's a bit of a shock."

"I can tell."

You're my first female pastor…Ordained woman?…Can you get married?…What do I call you, pastorette, pastoress, sister?…I've never seen anything like you…I have never heard a woman preach before now…You're a reverend? Such remarks were common in my first years of ministry. I thought they would cease over time. They did not. Recently, a woman in my writing class, seeing me walk in wearing my clergy collar, smiled with delight and exclaimed, "I've never seen this!" A smile is always better than a disapproving frown so I twirled so that my skirt flared and responded, "Ta dah!"

No doubt, a female pastor's presence arouses curiosity. By far the most frequent query from the curious has been, "How did you ever decide to become a pastor?" The second-most: "Is your husband a pastor, too?" A husband. Unexpected. Unanticipated. In my new life in Rome, I held on to a mere iota of hope regarding men. During my internship, I had stirred the ardor of a member of the parish who was a married man, and he had pursued me. I said no, naturally, but was disheartened that only an off-limits man wanted a relationship with me. Meanwhile, I was not even meeting available ones! Nor was I sure I wanted to. I had gotten burned badly only a few months before I had graduated from seminary.

I had dated a man from the second year class for a few months. I was not in love but was steaming toward it. He was so intriguing. Unbeknownst to me, I was the other woman. The lying weasel was engaged to be married in just a few months. When I found out, I got drunk to the point where my dry heaves were almost a near-death experience and my memory of the night was spotty. What a fool I had been to have let him suck me in.

"Everyone knows I'm engaged, Margie," he said.

"Well, not me, you toad. And you told me how special I was and how you could tell me anything. You're a lying shit." Were men even worth this?

When I moved to Rome, I expected more being-left-at-the-bar experiences, so I figured that I would most likely be single forever. That would be okay. I was determined that I'd create a pleasant, accomplished life and future. God would bless me, single or married.

Little did I know that back in my hometown, my future

was being innocently hatched by my mother, in collusion with Dave's mom. Oley, Pennsylvania, has stereotypical small-town relationships. People know each other and know what is going on in the lives of others. My mother went to the bank one day and Mabel, the outgoing redheaded teller, asked about me. Mom happily shared the news. "She's living in Rome, New York, serving her first church."

"Rome! My son, David, lives near there. He got out of the air force and moved there from Hawaii a few months ago. Here's his number. She can give him a call. I'll tell him about her."

When my mom told me about Dave my reaction was, "David Derr, no way." I remembered him as a party boy who not only drank but used drugs, too. Ah, but then, my total lack of a social life, other than church events, wore me down. I called him and invited him to my apartment in Rome for dinner. It was the evening when I wore the tube top he now remembers fondly, whereas I recall the flowers he brought and our conversation about high school and the parades in which we had both marched with the band. Surprisingly, I liked him.

He liked me as well and phoned me nightly. These calls resulted in laughter and easy get-acquainted conversations. "Can you go out to eat with me Wednesday?"

"No, I have an evening meeting."

"How about Thursday?"

"Sorry, a class that night."

"Well, I'm persistent. How about Friday?"

"Friday will work." It was the night that the pepper sauce

bottle shattered on the counter and ruined my dress. I said "shit," and a couple was born. The evening ended with a melting kiss at my front door.

What are you doing, Marjorie? You're just going to get hurt again. Don't do it. But there was "something about him" as they say. We had both grown up in Oley but had known little of each other in our developing years. In fact, I stayed away from him due to his wild streak. Two years ahead of me in school, Dave had been in the graduating class with my sister, Susie. We laughed when he told me how he had loved her in fourth grade. She had stabbed him in the back—literally—with her pencil. Such was true love for nine-year-olds. Dave still has the lead mark in his back from that Cupid's-arrow.

Remarkably, ten years post high school, while living 250 miles north of our hometown, we began to meld our lives. He had mended the renegade drinking and drug dabbling ways of his teen and young adult years and I had relaxed out of my Goody Two-shoes moralism. Consequently, as two people heading toward age thirty, we were happily dumbfounded that we clicked.

One evening, while at a restaurant in Utica, I looked at this stocky, redheaded, bearded man sitting across from me. His body was not the archetype of my dreams. I liked men trim and blond. Dave has shoulders like a linebacker. Yet, it didn't matter. "I can't believe I'm dating David Derr."

Dave reached for my hand and replied, "I can't believe I'm dating Marjorie Weiss."

"You really don't mind that I'm a pastor?"

"Not a bit. It's intriguing. What you do on a daily basis is fascinating. It's much more meaningful in the overall big picture of life than what I do."

"Computer programming sure is cutting edge stuff, Dave. Sounds important to me."

"Maybe, but not even close to being the same level of importance. What you do can change people's lives. This God stuff kinda mystifies me. But I've been reading up about Christianity—adult Christianity, not the Sunday school stuff I grew up with. Your work can't compare to mine."

"But your job…"

He cut me off. "This isn't a competition, Margie. You already won. I admire what you've accomplished; getting a master's degree is hard work. The air force *made* me learn programming."

"You're good at it, though."

"Yeah, but I wonder if it's what's right for me. I do think you may be right for me, though."

"Aren't you the charmer!" And he was.

No matter the subject: politics, books, television, or movies, we seemed simpatico. We both like Arthurian legends and *Star Trek*. We were readers: he loves fantasies, I love nonfiction. I was attracted to his confident manner, that he had a solid job, and was service-oriented. I was impressed that he had helped coach a girls' softball team when he lived in Hawaii at Hickam Air Force Base. And he was a formidable opponent in Scrabble. A smart man. I liked that.

Typically forthright, Pretend Margie nowhere to be found,

I shared my continuing self-image issues due to my teeth, and he assured me that I was beautiful to him. "Heck Margie, I once weighed 250 pounds—in seventh grade, no less. I'm the last one to judge anyone on self-image." He introduced me to his hobbies of record collecting and playing pool. I didn't tire of the enticing verbal pictures and stories he told of his three years in Hawaii. It sounded like paradise. This man was paradise to me.

Not three weeks into our relationship, we lay on the carpet of my apartment, listening to music emanating from my little cassette recorder. Dave reached over, kissed me and said, "I love you, Margie."

Danger, danger! Suddenly the robot from *Lost in Space* sounded a warning in my brain, addressed to Will Robinson but I knew it was meant for me. I began to cry.

"Aw, look at you. That makes you happy, that I love you?"

"I don't know. I'm more scared than happy. I wasn't expecting such words so soon."

"But it's how I feel…I love you."

"I've told you about my bad luck with relationships and the guy at seminary who was engaged. You don't have a woman waiting in the wings, do you?" I touched his cheek and looked at his face to try to tell if he was being truthful.

"I'm all yours." He covered my mouth with more kisses.

I laughed and gasped, "Be patient with me. Once burnt, twice shy, you know."

David was indeed patient and I gradually leaned into love with him. The biggest obstacle for me was his uncertainty about Christianity. Could I share a lifetime with a man who did not share my faith? Much to my great astonishment, I decided the answer was no.

"I can't see you anymore, Dave. I've fallen in love with you, but how can I be a pastor and be married to a man who doesn't pray or share my values of faith?" We were sitting on the sofa in my apartment, our bodies curved so we could face each other.

"But you know I've been reading lots about Christianity and I've been going to your church," he protested. "I like it there. You're a good preacher. I keep asking you all kinds of questions about it all. Even growing up in a church, I always had questions. Give me binary code, that is logical. This faith stuff mystifies me."

"Yeah, and I've told you, and told you, that I cannot be your Christian counselor! I'm emotionally involved and can't be unbiased. I've suggested many times that you go see Pastor Maier (a nearby Lutheran pastor) but you won't go. I just can't do this anymore. It's torture for me to see you and know we shouldn't be together."

"But we could be if you'd change your mind."

"I can't. I've wanted a man in my life. I've hoped for marriage, and here you sit, my dream come true. But my loyalty to Jesus tells me that to marry a non-Christian would just doom us. I'm more surprised than you could know about my decision. I can't believe that I actually feel this way. I must be nuts." He left with tears coursing down his cheeks. They matched mine.

I couldn't sleep that night. Dave tells me he didn't either. This crisis between us was the catalyst for David to finally go see Pastor Maier. Dave's main issue was that choosing to be

Christian would cut him off from other intellectual life choices. Pastor Maier helped him see that any choice supplants some things about the future, but opens up many new possibilities as well. "What could life with Jesus give you?" he asked him.

In one of our previous conversations about faith, I had told Dave about a fable I knew. It was about a rich, but shady character who had fallen in love with a beautiful, kindhearted woman. He knew she would never fall for the cruel person that he was. After all, his face clearly reflected his barbarous nature. So the man put on a lifelike mask, that of a man of mercy and care. While wearing the mask, his daily actions were those of a benevolent man. As a result, the woman readily fell in love with him. They married and their life was lovely in all ways except for the falsity of the mask. The lie he had to live, hiding his true, dark self finally became more than he could bear. He determined to take off the mask and show his wife who he really was. When he took it off he was astounded to see the face underneath had changed. He had actually transformed into the compassionate man whom he had been acting like all that time.

What would life with Jesus give Dave? Life with Jesus would give Dave *me*. That was his decision. I didn't know it at the time, nor likely did he, but he had chosen to wear the mask of faith, hoping it would transform him into the man he wanted to be for me—hoping it would result in a Christian faith of integrity. It never did.

A year and a day after our first date, Dave and I married joyfully in a church wedding in Oley in front of family and friends. There were eight pastors involved in our wedding. The pastor of my childhood church and my seminary preaching professor officiated together (both men), my seminary roommate, Mary, was a bridesmaid, and two clergy couples sang as a quartet. Number eight was me! We were elated to slide the wedding rings on each other's fingers. We had a bright future ahead.

Little did I realize that my wedding ring, a longed-for symbol of normalcy, would generate my best woman pastor story ever. I tell it often. Not long after our wedding, I was chatting with a patient during a pastoral visit in the intensive care unit at the hospital in Utica. Jack had a metal rod protruding out of both sides of his leg, which held it in traction. There was some dried blood around the rod, but nothing that gruesome, I'd seen much worse when visiting patients. I have a high yuck tolerance and try not to visually dwell on the grisly. My eyes seemed drawn to that rod however, and quite unexpectedly, I began to feel woozy. "Wow, Jack, I'm not feeling very well all of a sudden. I'm going to leave and perhaps can come back later."

As I pushed the button to automatically open up the ICU doors, blackness began to narrow my field of vision, a sure sign that I would faint. I had fainted a few times before—from a shot when I was a little kid at Doc Grimm's office, from the one time I tried to donate blood (convulsions with that one), and once when I sliced my thumb open and had watched the blood ooze. I usually stay upright when the trauma is on someone else, but when it is my body, I faint. It's always a miserable experience. I have naturally low blood pressure—often 90 over 56—so I don't have far to go to feel the blackness descend when my body feels threatened.

I was annoyed with it happening to me that day, but as I exited the ICU there was nothing to be done but ward off the event by lying down. A sure way to attract attention in a hospital is to lie down in the hallway. Soon enough I had a small group of hospital personnel above me. "Did you faint? Are you okay?"

"No, I didn't faint. I felt like I was going to faint so I lay down so I wouldn't."

"She fainted, get some smelling salts and a chair."

"No, I didn't faint. I was in ICU and..." I squeaked out as they put me on the chair and held vile smelling salts to my nose. One whiff and that did it. I passed into true I-feel-like-crap mode, worse than when I was on the floor. So much for my "helpers." Before I got another word in, beyond my moaning from the extreme wooziness the salts had brought on, there was a gurney by my side and hands assisting me to lie down on it.

"Are you pregnant? She must be pregnant."

"No, I'm not pregnant."

"I bet she's pregnant."

"No, I'm not, I just get this way sometimes from seeing blood. Really." They did not believe me.

After all the excitement, calming quiet descended when it was just me on the gurney in the elevator with the transport guy who was taking me to the ER. I had begun to feel better and knew it was just one of my near faints, but there I was, on my way to be checked out. I tried to loosen the clergy collar on my black blouse and as I did, Transport Guy must have noticed my left hand. "You wear engagement rings now, huh?"

"What?"

"You have an engagement ring on."

"What?" I was confused.

My obviously Roman Catholic transport guy said, "I thought nuns only wore wedding rings." (Through her vows, a nun enters a unique relationship with Jesus, based on her total dedication to him. She wears a wedding ring to symbolize marriage to Christ.)

"I'm not a nun, I'm a Lutheran pastor. I'm married to a man, not to Jesus."

"Oh." The rest of our trip to the ER was silent, my uniqueness having left him speechless. The ER doctors found, after some tests, that there was nothing wrong with me, other than that I almost fainted. I knew that all along. If only they had left me on the floor to stave off the wooziness, I would have saved a lot of money. But then I would have missed stunning that man to wordlessness.

Life for David and me was good. We were both happy with our companionship, he had even become involved in the youth ministry at our church. But neither of us was finding life in Rome very stimulating. Dave had been used to the built-in community of the air force and the city attractions of Honolulu and I, the seminary and Philadelphia. We found it difficult to find things to do and to meet people to become part of a social group. We intuitively knew that neither of us could be all things to the other and that friendships and individual interests were important. I plugged along, trying to be creative at both my congregations and hoping that I might form friendships with people I'd met in civic organizations or at my water aerobics class. I didn't. And of course, all my work nights out were quite the social hindrance.

Dave filled the gap by choosing to go back to college after a seven-year break and began studies toward a degree in English Literature. His busier schedule, however, brought us a new visitor: Mr. D! Although it would be fifteen years before that depressive scourge would be identified and the moniker given to it, he was very real. On Mr. D's visits, my husband would turn into a surly, negative fellow. "Why are you treating me this way, Dave? I don't get it. I haven't done anything to deserve this nasty tone." We talked and talked about it, unaware of the tentacles of depression that had begun to wrap themselves around Dave's spirit.

Those conversations circled similar subjects each time: "We have no friends." Dave said, "This split call of yours, juggling two churches and not reaching your potential in either of them, is not good for you, Margie. I don't like it."

I concluded, "Your unsettledness must be due to living in Rome, so let's get out of here and you'll be happier and not so touchy." Dave agreed. "Where shall we go?" I asked.

"I will follow you, Margie. Talk to the bishop and find

out what may be out there for you in a church. I'll find a job wherever you wind up."

"Things will surely be better when we move," I agreed.

Therefore, when the bishop told me of an opportunity at a larger church, I interviewed and got the job. We eagerly moved to Schenectady, New York, for my full-time call as Associate Pastor at a suburban congregation. Dave was going to work as a programmer for General Electric. It was November 1983, two years after our marriage.

Mr. D stowed away on the moving van, the clever bastard.

Three years later.

My heart rate was racing and my stomach was fluttering with nausea as I listened to the message my colleague, Pastor Charles, was delivering to the dozen children sitting at his feet before the altar step. I was "on" next. Steps. I stared at the four steps that led up to the pulpit. They may as well have been a mountain. *Can I keep from fainting? Why does this keep happening when it's my turn to preach? Suck it up, Marjorie, and get up there. People love your sermons. There's nothing to fear. You can do this.*

Something was obviously wrong. My body told me so.

The golden days that had been mine in my first years at the congregation outside Schenectady had tarnished. That was certain. When I began my work there, I immediately liked the pace. Everything was going great. There had been abundant things at the congregation to keep me busy and satisfied. "Team ministry" is what church folk call two clergypersons working together at the same congregation (often with additional staff people). I liked Charles, the Senior Pastor, and was glad to have a sounding board and someone to collaborate with. *It will not be so lonely here.*

Moving to a congregation with two services for three hundred people each Sunday was a stirring tonic for my spirit. An active place, the church was large enough for me to offer a class and actually get a sizeable group to show up. My work with the youth group was fun, especially the weekend retreats we held at an Adirondack mountain lodge.

Also fun and rewarding was gaining expertise in Christian sexuality education—sex ed—with a moral slant that public schools cannot provide. What an enjoyable challenge it was to research and learn about how to develop a curriculum. At one such class, I used charts and drawings to explain sexual intercourse to a group of fifth-graders, while their parents sat in the background. One boy eagerly raised his hand. "My parents only did it once."

The parents whooped and I quieted them as I asked, "Why do you say that?"

"Because I have one brother and I'm adopted." The parents' laughter was even louder.

"Oh, don't you mind those grown-ups. They're just surprised. I'm so glad you said that because I wasn't clear if you think intercourse is only for making babies. Husbands and wives make love because it is God's way for people to show their love and to grow closer to each other. I'm certain your parents have done it more than once." He looked back to them in question and they nodded in the affirmative. His aghast expression at this realization was priceless.

At the same time, I was also involved in starting and maintaining various "small groups." Such groups help people in congregations make friends and assimilate them into the congregation—everything from prayer groups to Mr. Fix-It squads. They are key to a congregation's growing and thriving. One group I started was for young adults. It met a need and developed into a social group for Dave and me as well. I still had the pastor label when I played volleyball or attended parties with that group, which was not ideal, but it was better than the dearth of friends we experienced in Rome. Dave and I were even the hit of the costume party one Halloween, dressed as Cindy Lauper and the wrestler she was managing at the time.

During the first few years at Good Shepherd I really enjoyed my work and people seemed to appreciate it, especially my preaching. I had developed into a very good storyteller and challenging speaker. I got one of my best compliments from a man who said, "You make us think of stuff we don't want to think about."

Dave was content with his work with GE. Not thrilled, but content. Mr. D. had remained at bay for the most part. We were taken with the area, living not far from the city, and enjoyed attending theater and concerts. We bought our first house and became do-it-yourselfers, working well together on home and yard improvement. Proudly we surveyed the lovely openness in the backyard after we took down thirty pine trees (that had been planted too closely together) all by ourselves. A neighbor even helped haul the branches to the road for pickup. *This is so much better than Rome. Neighbors talk to you.* Gradually though, the roses in Churchland wilted. Gray shadows took their place in the form of disgruntled parishioners who blindsided me.

Easter Day, the day to celebrate Jesus' resurrection from the dead, is always *the* grand day for Christians. It's a Sunday of filled-to-overflowing pews. How could I imagine such a day of celebration would result in sadness for me?

The pressure is on for the Easter preacher so I spent extra time that year on a just-right sermon. My sermon was entitled, *A Lily Among the Garbage.* I thought it was exceptional and I told the congregation the following tale.

> There are unique worship services led by mute clowns. At one such service, the confession of sins portion of the day was at the beginning, just like we do it. A clown was standing at a large garbage can. One by one he would pull a newspaper page from under his coat on which one word was printed in extra large black lettering… such as "war," "murder," "bullying," "gossip." As the clown held up the newsprint he encouraged the congregation with hand gestures to read out the word. With each new word he rallied them to be louder, thus confessing their sin. The clown ceremoniously put each newspaper in the garbage can, one by one. Then he put on the lid,

and with a big smile, put a potted Easter lily on top of the can. The lily represented forgiveness.

I continued by discussing the types of garbage in our world that need the transforming lily of God's new life—things like racism, rape, war, and the like. I was proud of the message and glad for the affirming comments from folks that said more than, "Nice sermon, Pastor." They seemed to get it: that resurrection is not just afterlife, but this-life.

Two days later a letter arrived at the church for the president of the Church Council with a copy for me. It was from George, a longtime member, complaining about how much of a downer my sermon had been. "People come to church on Easter wanting to be lifted up, not to hear things about the garbage of our world! You need to tell Pastor Weiss to stop doing such things. It will turn people away from our church." I was angry. I was hurt. I felt betrayed. I had thought that George and I got on well. I wrote back to him, defending myself, too chicken to talk to him face-to-face. I thanked him for his input although I noted that I disagreed and expressed chagrin that he did not speak to me personally. The council president also wrote to him and told him how my sermon had personally uplifted him. That was the end of it...other than in the part of my brain that hangs on to the negative. Why would a church member do that to me? I disliked the power it had over my being. It became a negative festering energy. Yet another cinder block was laid: I could not always trust church members.

I was glad to have finally made a few women friends in

the church. Now, how could something go wrong with a true friend? Connie, for example, was a new member of the church. We would visit each other and talk church of course, but we also wandered into conversations about gardening, handcrafts, travel, husbands, and life. Girl stuff. I loved it. Our friendship meant a lot to me. I trusted her. She never used our friendship to make herself look good in the church, understanding that it was best to not broadcast our relationship.

Unfortunately, Connie and her husband split up and I found myself walking with her, both as friend and pastor, through her grief and anger. As I learned, the lines can get blurred when a pastor has a friend in the parish. I discovered this when her husband unexpectedly made an appointment with me at my office. He wanted to discuss the impact of their pending divorce on their children. When Connie found out I'd met with him she phoned and angrily chided me. "This is a conflict of interest. You never should have talked with him!"

"I'm his pastor, too, Connie. I didn't betray any confidences or discuss anything that you told me. He just wanted to talk about the kids." My voice quavered as I tried to hold down my hurt at her unjust attack. She felt betrayed, but so did I.

"You never shoulda done it."

"And leave him with no pastor?"

"Yes, you could've referred him to someone else."

"But you know he's not keen on Charles, so who else, huh?"

"You could've found someone!"

"I don't know what to say except I'm really sorry you feel this way. Really sorry. If this affects our friendship, it's your choice and not mine." It did. She cut me off. I was more than sad, a feeling exacerbated by the way she would silently walk by me on Sunday mornings. I knew I had done the right thing pastorally, but was not sure I had done the right thing for my now former friend.

Another incident that stabbed at my spirit for a long time was the ongoing icy brusqueness I received from June, a mother of two young children. She had phoned me one Sunday afternoon to castigate me about the children's message I had given that day at worship. Here is what I had told the kids:

"So what's the fastest animal? Does anyone know?...A cheetah, that's right. Here's a picture of one. If a cheetah and a man run a race around the outside of the church, who would win?...The cheetah, of course. But how about if a cheetah and a man run a race all the way to your house and back? Who would win? The man, because humans can run farther than a cheetah in a long distance race. But the man has to practice to be a strong runner. Our lesson from the Bible today says a friendship with Jesus takes work. It takes practice. How can we practice so we can have our friendship with Jesus be strong? Sunday school, prayer, worship...Good answers! Yes, even doing things for others is good practice. Super. See you next week!"

June was icy and smug when she spoke to me and pointedly corrected me. "When you tell the children something, it needs to be the truth. You told them a lie about that cheetah. A cheetah would win a race with a human. How can you expect the children to learn anything from you about faith when you lie like that?" I couldn't believe it. I sputtered out my defense that my facts were accurate, which she did not accept, so I took my licking. There was no Google to prove my point. (Google does confirm that a cheetah would lose a race with a human of at least four miles length, so take that June!) I conjectured that there was a deeper dissatisfaction that had led to June's anger, but what else was I to do? Even all these years later, whenever I go to a zoo and view a cheetah, June is there, too. Surely the cheetah sees my dour expression and wonders, "What did I ever do to you?"

Three decades older and now more seasoned as a pastor, I am keenly aware that being blindsided by disgruntled parishioners is common. I hate it. I really hate it. I would go along from day to day, saying and doing things I felt were positive and professional, unaware that someone was upset by something I couldn't possibly have predicted was an upset-able thing. Then, pow, I would get the phone call or e-mail, or worse, the message through a third party. "Pastor, did you know that so and so is really mad because..." When a person can't even talk to me, but talks about me, I want to bite something the way my cat does when she's mad. It wore on me in each occurrence. Each incident was a building block of cinder and I knew it not.

Obviously, being blindsided affected me adversely, especially when it was not counterbalanced in my subconscious by the many positives at the congregation. Further heightening overall stress for me was the souring of team ministry. I had expected it to help me be less isolated. The opposite was the reality. Team ministry is like a marriage: when you are not in love, it can be arduous. With Charles and me, it became so. He and I had differing temperaments and styles. I had ideas that did not match his and since he was the senior pastor, I had to defer, even when I did not agree. That dynamic detracted from the enjoyment of our work for both of us.

My sermon-nausea continued for several months. The results of the tests my doctor ordered told me nothing was physically wrong. It must be psychological. A counselor gave me guidance in dealing with the bothersome frustration. She helped me see that my nausea was a symptom of anger I didn't even know was brewing. Once I became more aware of what pushed my buttons, the nausea abated. However, I remained a simmering kettle of disappointment.

Work life was not ideal, but home life was soon to get happily stimulating. We became parents. We had not planned long for adoption. It was not part of any plan actually. In 1986 a boy at the church had become orphaned and Dave and I seriously considered taking him in. He did find a new home with others, but his predicament was the root of our investigating the possibility of adopting an older child. Not keen on trying to conceive a baby at that time—how would we ever fit that into our busy days and all my nights out?—we thought an older child, already in school, might work for us. Helping a child in need appealed to us both. My counselor agreed with me that motherhood might lead me into a better balance between work and personal life.

We were pleased when New York State Social Services approved us to adopt. Newly available kids could be viewed in bi-monthly photo listings. Look at a photo. Read a short paragraph about the child. Throw your names into the hat for those of interest. And so, we began to apply for girls who caught our interest as Dave leaned toward girl more than boy. We always got a photo of the child to take home which we put into a file and then forgot about it, knowing not to get attached to any of the children.

We heard not one response from our dozens of inquiries until nine months later—ironic, no? We were told more about a child, one of the many in our pile of photos, named Lynn, whose social worker thought might be a good fit for us. The day we met our soon to be, not-at-all shy child, we took her to a local burger joint and ordered milkshakes. Her dirty blond pixie haircut framed a slender face with bright blue eyes as she told us about her favorite music and how the chocolate shake made her "taste bugs" dance. Dave's eyes crinkled in a smile as they met mine. Lynn glowed when we showed her the photo of the brand new bed and matching dresser that awaited her a month later when she would move in with us. Then Lynn got quiet.

"What's up?" I asked. "It looks like something's bothering you."

Lynn covered her mouth with her hand. "I'm gonna need braces. That costs money." Her forehead furrowed with concern. "Do you still want me?" She was endearingly blunt. Her eyeteeth were erupting above the lateral incisors. She was definitely right about those braces.

"We can afford to get you braces," Dave responded while squeezing my hand. "That's what parents do for their children."

"Well, my last parents told me they wouldn't get them for me." She paused, took another sip of her shake and said, "Thanks for adopting me."

We'd been told Lynn's history. We thought we knew what we were getting into, but after she moved in, her deep pain oozed like a bleeding wound. Lynn's birth parents had been unable to care for her when she was a toddler so she had been placed into foster care. The foster parents adopted her, raising her on a farm with their biological daughter. One day, Lynn heard her father call social services and say, "Come and get her. We don't want her anymore. Bring a big car so all her stuff goes with her." She was three months past her eighth birthday.

Officially called an adoption disruption, the greatest disruption was in the psyche of that child. We were told to anticipate her being angry. Of course, she was deeply wounded. How could she not be with that rejection?

I saw the hand of God at work because from 120 families who had expressed interest in her, they had chosen us. We were thrilled. So was the church. Women there threw a "baby" shower for our size ten, 60-pound baby, a week before the big move. Therefore when Lynn arrived in March 1987, she walked down the steps to our family room to see the piles of clothes and toys. "Are these all for me?" The wonderment on her face was touching, considering that the clothes she had when she arrived were really crap, their poor condition screaming how devalued she had been with her former parents. The girl was staring at heaven.

Lynn was a dear little girl and together we ventured to form a family unit. We got to know Sunshine, the one toy from her former life, a stuffed dog who slept with her and joined us in evening prayers. She eased into calling us Mommy and Daddy. Dave and I were initially dazed and dog-tired from the taxing transition into instant parenthood at our ages of thirty-one and thirty-three. We had not imagined the stress or fatigue. However, it was good stress, different stress. One of the most difficult things for us was the endless number of times we had to say no.

"Can I watch TV until 10:00pm?"

"No."

"I want to ride my bike farther than the end of the street."

"No."

"I want ice cream for dessert every night."

"No."

When you don't have the child from day one, the word "no," something parents often say to protect and teach, did not feel nice. What a learning experience this turned out to be.

The "compliant child" honeymoon period lasted about three weeks. Lynn's unspoken, subconscious question was, "When will these new parents kick me out, too?" Hence, the testing began.

As a second-grader, her reading was poor, so her new teacher asked us to have her read out loud each night. One evening she sat on my lap at the dining room table as she read. Her sandy hair smelled of salon from her hair cut that day and her frame was light. She'd read a sentence or two and I would correct her as needed. The more I corrected her pronunciation, the more I saw the steam coming out of her ears. "Mom, you are really bugging me and I am about to have a temper tantrum." We had heard of these tantrums from her social worker. Lynn had even been medicated for a time since she would get so "out of control." Dave and I, with doctor's approval, had taken her off that medication, wanting to assess her from a clean slate.

"Well, go ahead, I'd like to see one," I responded, never expecting what was to follow. Dave, close by in our living room also witnessed the well-orchestrated, obviously well-practiced tantrum. Lynn jumped from my lap and began kicking things, knocking over a chair. The adult language that she uttered would have impressed a sailor. In an attempt to calm her down, Dave wrapped her in his arms and promptly got kicked as Lynn tried desperately to get him to release her. He sat down on the sofa, clinging tightly to her body.

"Let me go! Let me go! I hate you!" Our neighbors across the street probably heard her.

Dave, who over the coming months became proficient in holding her that way in similar bouts, said what would become a mantra she needed to hear, and learned eventually to believe, "I love you too much to let you go." At least thirty minutes went by with her battling and declaring her hate and our countering with words of love. It was a stupendous event for us as new parents. Dave did not let her go. Lynn finally exhausted herself and began to cry.

"Are you calm enough that I can let you go now, Lynn?" he asked.

Whimpering, she nodded her head and was released. She came to me, wrapped her arms around me, and sobbed, "I'm sorry. I'm sorry, Mommy. I'm sorry, Daddy."

"We're sorry, too, kiddo. That's quite a big deal over reading a story," Dave said as he approached us for a family hug. "How about you get ready for bed, and then we'll talk about it when we say bedtime prayers."

We were bone-weary, especially poor Dave whose arms had gone numb, but Lynn smiled and loped up the stairs as if nothing had happened. We looked at each other and simultaneously agreed, "Out of control, nothing. She knew exactly what she was doing." And she did. Lynn was trying to take control of a world that had treated her like she was garbage to be tossed out. That tantrum was her way of declaring: I am worth something, so don't you mess with me.

Not long afterward, on a summer day we traveled to a picnic. Lynn was heartily steamed as she sat in the back seat, really mad that we had not let her wear sandals. "No, it's safer for you when you run and play to wear your sneakers."

"I want my sandals!"

"No, it will be your sneakers." Back and forth we went until an exasperated Dave picked her up and lightly tossed her into the back seat of the car.

She was mightily pissed off at that. As we drove, she attacked. "I'm gonna call the cops on you fucking assholes." Since that got no reaction, she used her fingernails. On my arm. Dave was driving so she knew not to attack him, but I was fair game on the passenger side. Blood began to drip from the gashes she left. I yelled for her to stop while she yanked the strap of my tank top and ripped it straight through.

"What do you want to do, Margie?" Dave said loudly over Lynn's voice. He was trying to remain calm enough to drive. "Just keep going to the picnic, we're almost there. I'll ask them for a T-shirt to put on." Lynn then ripped the other strap off. We arrived shortly after, Dave got a T-shirt from our host, and we went to the backyard for the picnic, but Lynn refused to go. She stood in the garage and pouted. About ten minutes later, after I had bandaged my arm, we went out to check on her. She ran to me crying.

"I'm sorry, Mommy. I'm really sorry. I was just mad, too mad."

"Of course, I forgive you, but Daddy and I will discuss the consequences of this when we get home and let you know what your punishment is. You just can't do stuff like this. Now come out to the backyard and play with the other kids." She had a nice time and it was wise that she had on those sneakers.

Interestingly, after that incident, our household became more peaceful. The family counselor we had been seeing surmised, "Lynn's been as bad as she has ever been and you've still kept her, so now she feels more secure. That's why she doesn't act out as often anymore. It was a test she didn't even know she was administering. I'd say you passed." Hallelujah! was our reaction to a calmer household.

Raising Lynn was more challenging than we had expected, but the counselor told us we were "masterful" at it, seeming to know instinctively how to handle the challenges she presented us. That led us to feel more confident.

Before the adoption, Mr. D had been lying in dormancy. Let-me-alone-you-annoying-wife was the vibe Mr. D would sometimes give off so I would keep my distance. But mostly, Dave was happy, engaging, and social. He enjoyed our events with other young adults at church. He was an involved husband. I could depend on him. But Mr. D stealthily began to use our relationship with Lynn as an opportunity to entrap Dave in growing negativity. We were still unaware of the depression's existence. I just knew my husband was increasingly surly and down, his face a mask, and he was becoming more physically remote from me and Lynn. It seems both mother and daughter were annoying. I didn't like that his moodiness bled onto our child. It unsettled her, and me. He began to gain weight, too.

Nevertheless, most days were happy and fulfilling. I liked parenting. Third grade moved into fourth. She rode her bike farther. She was invited to parties. She had two girlfriends in the neighborhood with whom to share secret things. It was all normal kid stuff. Although we were unsettled by the occasional tantrums that showed Lynn's psychological anxiety, Dave no longer had to clutch her in his arms.

Then we did something wonderful. We conceived a child. At the time we found out, we were blissfully ignorant of the effect that the increased responsibilities would later have on a (yet undiagnosed) depressed man. Those nine months led to mixed emotions for our ten-year-old. Lynn was happy and excited about the baby one day while on the next, that baby was her enemy, especially after we found out we were having a girl. "Why can't it be a boy? You'll love this new sister more, just like my old parents loved their real daughter more than me. They kicked me out, but she got to stay."

We countered with things like: "This is your forever home, Lynn. You're our real daughter. We have enough love for both you and your coming baby sister. We're sure you'll make a terrific big sister. We'll always love you no matter what. We are not like your former parents." (Shockingly, more than one person at church asked if we were going to give Lynn back since we were now having our "own" child.)

Eight months into what had been a physically very easy pregnancy, Lynn was mad about something—she had a short fuse, still does—when she yelled, "I hate you. I hate the baby, too!" I knew she was just acting out, but I hauled my big belly and hormonal emotions up the stairs to by bedroom and fell in a sad heap on the bed. *How is this ever going to work? What were we thinking?* I was thirty-five. *Too old? Would we be able to manage a baby and a tween-aged Lynn?*

Angela's birth, however, turned out to be a gift to our family. It gave Dave, Lynn and me something that we all shared from the beginning. I asked Lynn a few years ago what had helped her get over the threat she had felt as we awaited Angela's birth. "When I saw that you didn't treat me any differently, I knew it would be okay," was her response. She enjoyed the baby. I think this surprised her.

Unexpectedly, Angela's existence also made me fit in. How wonderful was that? When I attended my new mom's group and baby swim classes I was part of normal things. I was just like the other mothers: breastfeeding, spending nights up with the baby, changing diapers, pushing strollers, installing car seats, smelling baby smells, and just plain enjoying the overall pleasure of seeing our baby grow and change.

After Angela's birth in 1989, I gladly left my job. I needed a break from ministry and the small group of testy people who had soured the stew. I'd been there six years and felt blessed that we could afford for me to become a stay-at-home mother for the girls. What a singular time for me and for our family: quieter days of cooking, sewing, attending school events, and volunteering. Mr. D, however, roamed our house and really grabbed hold when Dave was laid off from his programming job and we had no income. Our family was comprised of a stay-at-home-mom, a nine-month-old baby, an almost-sixth-grader, and a man with anxiety about being unemployed. It was peachy. For Mr. D, at least. Dave's negative flare ups changed the tone of our house, but when my cajoling did not work, a smiling baby coaxed him out of it. She would look at him with her bald headed, Gerber-baby face, grin ear to ear, crawl toward him, and miraculously, Dave's demeanor would get gooey and soft. Mr. D, who does not like babies, would run.

One of us needed to find full-time work. We both looked and he got a programming position just two weeks before unemployment compensation would have stopped. Thank you, God. But he was not happy in that job. Depression does that to a person: making the forecast for the future of one's vocation always seeming to be cloudy and rainy. However, we still were unaware of Mr. D so I just stewed about it, and instead fantasized about what life could be like with a happy man.

Two years later, I was hankering to get back to work, seeking more stimulation than a toddler, a middle-schooler, and domestic pursuits could provide. Yeah, I knew that a new church for me would be populated with the grand old souls, as well as people I would want to kick in the ass, but optimistic, ambitious Margie was looking for a challenge. *I'll develop a thick skin this time around when I feel betrayed.* Dave looked forward to a change from his unfulfilling job and said, as before, "Your work takes the lead for where we go next." A new beginning would be good for Dave and would surely get him out of his funk since we decided he would be a stay-at-home dad for a few years. *Surely, that will make him happy.* (Mr. D. howled happily when I said that.)

"Where shall I look?" I inquired.

"How about a small town this time?"

"Really, why?"

"Remember how people were connected in Oley when we were growing up?" Dave had loved the annual fair and I saw his eyes gleam from the memory of volunteering there.

I agreed that an actual town might give us a place, not just to domicile, but that would feel like home. So, I sent my professional application to a bishop in Pennsylvania who set me up for an interview at a congregation in an upstate river town called Danville. I knew of it because it was not far from the college I'd attended. The other applicants were men, but I got the job. That was exciting and affirmed that I was viewed as having the skills to lead a congregation on my own, despite my gender. The year was 1992 and I was thirty-eight.

Danville became our new home, but unfortunately it was not to be Home.

Pastorette

Our new home was a medium-sized river town in the north-central part of Pennsylvania. I was elated to have been called by God to work there. It had what I had been looking for in a congregation: diversity in ages, families, children, youth, and senior citizens, as well as people with an expressed desire to grow in service to others. No longer an associate pastor, I looked forward to captaining the ship and setting a welcoming tone. Dave was indeed a stay-at-home dad (for almost two years) and later took a job as a computer programmer for a small business.

I served Trinity Lutheran Church for twelve years. The congregation thrived. It was a good fit between pastor and people. Right out of the gate the folks had to get used to their first female pastor, but a member named Harry told me, "I didn't want a woman pastor and voted against your coming, but as soon as I met you, I changed my mind." I was the only female pastor in a town of twenty Christian congregations of various denominations. That helped make Trinity unique and the congregants seemed pleased by that notoriety.

Most appreciated was my pastoral manner. Early on, Raymond, a long-time member, stopped by my office. He was a retiree who had worked for years in maintenance. "You know, Pastor, I want to tell you that I think you're doin' a hell of a job for us. The best thing is that you don't lord it over us; you're one of us. That sermon on Sunday was the best one I ever heard in all my years, and you know I've been around!" I laughed because he'd told me some stories from his time in the army so I knew what "been around" meant. And his saying hell in front of me was disarming. *Maybe I can be me, here.* I surely was going to try.

A purely subjective theory I have developed of congregations is that they gradually take on a corporate personality that begins to mirror their pastor. Formal pastors breed formal congregations; relaxed pastors lead to a congregation with that ethos. I was not overly formal in worship style, being more progressive in attitude and in contemporary worship style. In time, Trinity began to become more like me. Our worship had an experimental atmosphere with variety and included elements such as dance and drama presentations. We once hosted the "Biggest Banana Split in Danville" street festival for the community. The Sunday school grew in attendance each week. Several hundred new people joined the congregation. My idealism and compassion led us to start a community soup kitchen in 1993 that continues to operate today. Gay people found a home at Trinity. I enjoyed gratifying years of mentoring five interns from seminary who gave me companionship in ministry that heartened me. I led the congregation in a capital fund drive toward a very necessary addition to the church building. For a congregation with no debt since 1948 that was a tough sell, but folks eventually understood the need to update and expand the facilities in order to be ready for the twenty-first century.

Starting a Saturday evening contemporary worship service had the biggest impact on the congregation's ability to provide spiritual care since many people worked Sundays. We also hoped the Saturday night option would draw new people to the congregation, and it did. In particular, it drew one of God's very special people.

The week before the inaugural Saturday service, I was in town enjoying the annual Spring Fling with Lynn and Angela when someone called out my name. The voice was female, from what I could tell. It was piercing but without a menacing tone. I looked across the street, searching the faces. The crowd was large on Danville's main street. The May day was warm and the walkways cheerfully appointed with spring tulips and daffodils. The traffic had been detoured around the main drag which led to the bridge crossing the Susquehanna River. Both lanes were transformed into a street fair with vendors marketing their crafts, jewelry, food, and artwork.

The voice echoed again. How was I supposed to see who was calling me through the booths and canopies that lined the street? Fifteen-year-old Lynn, four-year-old Angela, and I had enjoyed some lunch from the vendors and then had perused the wares. Lynn had bought a necklace while Angela had been proud of the cat toy she had purchased with her own money for our two kitties at home. We'd had fun, a remarkable feat when combining Lynn's then teenage aloofness and Angela's frenetic preschool fidgeting. However, curly blond Angela had reached the limit of her attention span and it was time to go home. The unknown person called to me again as we were walking to the car. I saw Lynn's long straight hair whip around as she rolled her eyes and said, "It's another person from church, I bet. How many have we run into today already?"

"It's not a big town so of course, they'll be here. Besides, Simon from church bought you both homemade fudge, didn't he? People like to take care of the pastor's kids."

"Yeah, but I'm tired. Can't we go home?" Angela leaned into her sister's arm in agreement.

"We will. I just have to find out who's calling me."

"Whoever it is, she sounds like another one of your loons, Mom."

"What's a loon, Sissy?" Angela's interest was piqued.

"You know how Mommy's a pastor. Loon is a word for some of the weird people Mom runs into through the church," was Lynn's quick reply to her sister. "There's a lot of them!"

"Oh, now," I said to both of them, "the church welcomes everybody even if they don't fit in someplace else. Some people are just different." Then I whispered, "You know I don't like that word very much, Lynn. Not in front of your little sister."

"Yeah, but some of the people are just...loons." I smiled at her smirk, knowing it was true at Trinity just as it was in all churches; in all places, in fact.

The voice again lifted over the noises on the street. "Are you Marjorie Weiss? Are you Marjorie Weiss?" Finally, I saw her as she began to cross the street toward me. She was a sturdy, square woman, maybe mid-thirties, who walked with a gait not unlike a pregnant woman's waddle. As she neared I could tell that she was not pregnant. Her hair hung limply and her face shone from sweat and with happy expectation. "Are you Marjorie Weiss?" Her voice was loud even though she was almost next to us.

I smiled warmly and extended my hand. "Yes, I am. And what's your name?"

As she took my hand she surprised me by stooping over to kiss it and then rose and curtsied. "My name is Marlene. I saw your picture in the paper. But you're wearing blue jeans. You had on a black shirt in the paper. You are a very pretty girl."

My daughters observed Marlene with great curiosity. "Why, thank you. I'm glad you noticed the article. It was about the Saturday night worship service that is starting next week."

"Can I take you out for ice cream?" was her next question. *Where did that come from?* Marlene was indeed atypical.

"Uh, *now*?" I asked and Marlene nodded as she swayed from side to side.

"Oh, no thank you, Marlene. That's very sweet of you to offer, but my daughters, Lynn and Angela," I said, turning towards them, "are tired and we need to be getting home. But thank you for the invitation."

"Oh...okay." Marlene was disappointed. "How about tomorrow?" Angela actually put her hands over her ears. We had to get going.

"I'm so sorry, but no. Sundays are a busy day for me. Nice to have met you, Marlene. We have to go now. I hope I'll see you again."

"You remind me of my school nurse, Mary Jane Bridy. But you're a pastorette. I like that." She turned and skipped away. "I'll see you later, Marjorie Weiss. Goodbye, Pastorette. Next Saturday at church, I'll be there."

Lynn stood there holding Angela's hand with her mouth agape. "Wow, she sure was loud. And what's a pastorette?"

"There is no such word." (The only time I'd heard the word before was from men who wanted to make themselves feel tall by diminishing me as an ordained woman. I didn't want to tell Lynn that and give her a negative image of a church person.) "You girls were very patient. Thank you. Now, let's go home and tell Daddy about the fling."

Lynn just shook her head and muttered quietly, "Another loon!"

"She seemed sweet," I countered. "Unusual, but sweet."

The Saturday evening services took off. I was so pleased that they became popular. Informal in format, they appealed to not only members but also to the hoped-for new people. Our newspaper advertising encouraged casual dress, saying, "Join us Saturday nights. Come as you are." Ours was the only Protestant Saturday service in town so we had a corner on the market, so to speak.

Marlene was a regular worshipper on either Saturday or Sunday for the next ten years of my tenure at Trinity. She would always sit in the back pew, rocking back and forth. She often talked too loudly but I'd learned how to lower her volume with a touch or a gentle word. She was childlike, but the weekly letters, and the cards she sent me for every single holiday throughout the year, indicated that she was quite literate and an excellent speller.

Early in our relationship, she began to phone me at home regularly, often when I was in the middle of some family necessity like cooking. As a result, I came up with a plan I hoped would lay boundaries without offending her. "Marlene, how can friends like you and I find the time to have a good conversation on the phone? I have an idea! You can call me on Friday afternoons, but just on Fridays. Then I'll have time to talk. Do you think that will work?"

"Okay. Can I have a hug?" She leaned in for a hug which was followed by one of her light kisses on my cheek. Thereafter Marlene would call almost every Friday, tell me some marvelous thing about other women in other churches she knew or of the new drawing she had ready to show me. She loved to draw my cartoon face or figure next to the faces of other women who had been part of her life. Even to this day, I continue to receive drawings and holiday cards from her in the mail and I still get occasional phone calls. My cartoon face has not aged and my hair is still brown, so I really like that.

No doubt, Marlene is special. I was so pleased that the people at Trinity treated her with kindness. Obviously, they saw her devotion to me. How could they not, since I was the topic of each and every conversation she had with them? She was my biggest fan, bar none.

One day, the church custodian approached me at my office with a grin and began to laugh.

"What's so funny?"

Ed ran his hand through this graying hair as he spoke. "I saw your name on Mill Street the other day."

"On Mill Street? Where? Why?"

"I stepped on it!" Ed couldn't control his amusement as his shoulders shook with laughter. "Right there on the sidewalk in front of the Old Hardware Restaurant was written in chalk, 'I love Pastor Marjorie Weiss. She is a good girl.' "

"Marlene!"

Ed nodded his head. "The whole town knows about you and her now!"

"Free publicity is free publicity, Ed," I laughed.

"She sure is something, but you know I'd miss her if she stopped coming to church."

"So would I, Ed. I really would."

Pastorette. It was not a term that I would have embraced when I attended seminary. Those had been the early days of ordained women so it was important to be seen on equal footing with men. However, the enchanting Marlene has helped me redefine the title to a positive one.

Despite professional success and the many wonderful people at Trinity who loved me, the town was not to be a place of deep community for me. Dave and I hadn't realized how much we would miss being close to the goods and services we had had in Schenectady, as well as the cultural things that a city has to offer.

Friendships beyond church acquaintances were not to be. One would think that through our girls' activities we would have made connections with other parents, but no. That pastor label, again, was the cause. I was sure of it. We also discovered that many people in town still had friends from high school or extended family in the town. Hence, our theory was that they didn't need to reach out to newcomers.

Additionally, we were mightily challenged by adolescent Lynn. We had moved to Pennsylvania when she was entering eighth grade, and she was now about to enter high school. Her teeth were straight and beautiful. She was pleasantly curvy. She'd made friends in town, and it seemed like a promising ninth grade for her, as eighth had been filled with making good grades, playing in the school orchestra (string bass), and spending time with decent friends. Sadly, the brightness of grade eight dimmed during the transition into high school. We despaired as we watched her spiral downward, resulting in episodes of cutting, two "mild" suicide attempts and the failure of multiple friendships. However, she persevered at finding a life worth living, anger keeping her strong, willing her to survive. The toll on Dave and me was at times vast, much more painful than we had ever expected when we took that sweet little girl into our home. Her pain was ours. Our pain was each other's and there was little we could do other than survive.

I don't regret having Lynn as my daughter—far from it. I am proud of her and what she has accomplished as she is now a competent woman with an MBA. She's also a wife and a dedicated mama bear of a mother to her two kids. However, those teen years were a lonely walk for Dave and me. Through those years of parenting trials, I only met one other couple who could understand what Dave and I dealt with, a couple who also had adopted an older child. They knew the turmoil and anguish of feeling out of control, despite trying everything, and of being unable to help your child. Other folks said "helpful" things like: "She's a kid, she'll get over it... Oh, teenagers, they put you through the wringer, don't they? Don't worry, it's just a phase she's in." Yet, no one understood the depth of sorrow and concern we had for our wounded child. Their blithe aphorisms were unintentionally belittling.

Mr. D reveled in our travails. He made Dave increasingly unhappy with his programming job, increasingly unhappy with his home life, increasingly unhappy with me. It was a bleak time in our marriage with moments of utter blackness. Years later, when Dave and I sat at the Marriott restaurant before his DBS surgery he had asked me, "Would you have married me if you knew I would get Parkinson's Disease?" It was those Danville years that led to my answer, "Parkinson's yes. Depression, no."

Mr. D was living quite fiendishly in my husband. Lynn was

struggling. I was struggling. Angela was the sunshine. How she was not more affected at that time by the cloudy weather of our family, I do not know. This bleakness was ongoing throughout her preschool and elementary school years and yet, Angela was happy, delightful, and joyous. Her teachers always noted her ready smile and how she was a natural leader in class. She was social and was enlivened whenever she was with other children at daycare, Brownies, Sunday school, school, and children's choir. She sang as she walked around the house. She would snuggle in Lynn's bed, her tousled blond curls a halo around her goofy look-what-Sissy-and-me-are-doing grin. Angela very naturally offered all three of us unconditional love, and hence, a break from the tension. Mr. D did not appreciate that at all. Sadly, he now visits adult Angela far too often.

In addition to the family travails, normal work stresses mounted. I became the victim of my own success. The increases in church membership and activities kept me very busy. Too busy. And unfortunately, some of the church members had turned out to be mean, or sick, or even evil. Who needs that? The mason of the Cinder Block Room, of course.

Sticky relational issues at church began to burden me and I became less and less able to let things roll off my back. The same things that had upset me in Rome and Schenectady—people dealing poorly with conflict and being snarky and unkind to me and others—recycled themselves in similar scenes, just different actors. A couple who had been very involved with the congregation at Trinity left and would not tell me why…A staff person was maligning me behind my back and I had to confront him about it…A man got angry and quit all his volunteer work because I walked by him one Sunday morning and didn't say hello, no matter that I had not even seen him…A woman got upset enough to badmouth me around the church because I had not prayed with her grandson when he was a patient at the hospital, remaining upset even after I explained that they had taken him for X-rays before I had a chance…Another staff person got offended by something I said and stopped talking to me, the cold shoulder being my only signal that she was upset…A parent ignored the requirements for her child's confirmation class and was angry when I was not okay with that since "churches should be relaxed and not have expectations"…The finance committee didn't support me in a decision we had made together about increasing our church's contributions to charities…Person A got pissed off with Person B and came to me to fix it, without having had the courage to discuss the situation with Person B…Person C hauled off and humiliated Person D at a meeting and would not try to reconcile, but just quit…Person E, Person F, Person G, etcetera, etcetera. Those kinds of people issues were constant. Constant.

"Grow up, people!" I wanted to scream. "Be the Christians you proclaim you are." But instead, I had to "make nice." I took my responsibility to maintain the health and conviviality of the body of Christ seriously, knowing that if I did not handle these issues delicately that I might be the reason for someone leaving the congregation, or even worse, for them losing their faith. It is often the correct thing for a pastor to do: to eat his/her emotions to preserve the church. My problem was that I had developed no outlet to vomit them up later and rid myself of the anxiety and distress caused by holding them in.

My harshest critic was a vocal detractor who regularly sent me anonymous hate mail. After I left the congregation I found out who it was and can confidently refer to the writer as she, but during those years I had no idea. Her mail to the church was always typed on a typewriter, even the addressed envelope. Given that technologies such as Word, e-mail, and of course writing by hand, had been around for some time, it was apparent she went to some length to disguise herself. Among the things she sent me were:

- A cut-out of the ad for our Saturday evening service we'd put in the local newspaper. The ad was a photo of a pair of sandals and the words, "Jesus didn't care what people wore for worship, neither do we. Join us Saturday nights at 6:30pm." My hater's attached typed critique was: "Trying to bring in all sorts of odd people while not wearing a robe to lead worship! How liberal can a pastor get?"

- I had mentioned my cats in a church newsletter article so she sent me a coupon for kitty litter with a note that read, "Buy some litter and scoop up the shit that comes from your mouth."

An occasion arose that gave her the opportunity to publicly smear me. One Sunday in my sermon I used balloons as an illustration. I physically brought them, handed them out, and we batted them around the church. It was fun. People understood my point, which was that they needed to "blow" God's love to others and let God take it where it needed to go. I was really pleased with it and the smiles and nods indicated that it had worked. A few days later my hater phoned in an anonymous comment to the editor of the local newspaper, complaining about what I had done. Such comments appeared in a sound off column called "Thirty Seconds." She said: "Did anyone ever hear of passing out balloons at a church service and telling the congregation to blow up the balloons and bat them around in church? What kind of minister would do something like this? This was done recently at Trinity Lutheran Church. In the house of GOD. Shame on someone."

The editor responded: "I don't know for sure, but it seems likely the minister did it to illustrate some point *he* was trying to make. If that be the case, what's the harm? Organized religion is engaged in a desperate battle for people's hearts and minds. Churches are competing with all kinds of distractions and entertainment, created for the amusement of the richest society in the history of the world. What's wrong with a little showmanship to make a point?"

I wrote a letter that was published as my response, glad to let it be known I was a she:

> "Indeed, I used it as an illustration for Pentecost Sunday, the day Christians celebrate the presence of God and the Holy Spirit in the world. A balloon without air in it cannot do its job of bringing happiness to others. So it is with a Christian without the Holy Spirit. Since the Spirit is known as the breath of God, those at worship were invited to blow up their balloons to show the power that comes to the balloon. Batting them around was to show how kind actions and loving deeds can touch the lives of others in a snowball effect. I bear no ill will to the caller, have prayed for him or her and would hope the Spirit sends them a 'balloon' of kindness and the love of God."

Needless to say, this evil—for that is the best way to describe such hate—was like a leaky spigot that dripped acid on me, burning my spirit. I tried to ignore it and focus on the positives. The congregation was, overall, a good place to work. It was growing in size and activities. I was doing a good job.

Then the roof caved in. My Lutheran clergy colleagues betrayed me.

~

I had been in a years-long evolution in my beliefs regarding sexual morality. My conflicted feelings all those years ago about my everything-but-intercourse relationship with Tony had been the original prompt. It bonded us. Was it wrong? That experience, as well as my discussions with my gay seminary friend, began to move me toward a less resolute assessment of what is sexually right or wrong in the "eyes of God." Those sexual behaviors that I had been taught were sinful gradually moved into a less black-and-white area in my mind.

The controversial issue that continued to arise in congregations I served was homosexuality. More conservative Christians teach that "homosexual sex is a choice from which one needs to repent." Or, that "one can be gay, but cannot act on it as that is sin. Scripture is 'clear' on that point." Now, of course, we have legalized same-sex marriage in the United States. I was living through the difficult evolution towards that. Still, today many Christians continue to give the message that if you are gay you are going to hell. Such loveless-ness and the negative image it portrays of God makes me heartsick.

In the year 2000, eight years into my work at Trinity, I had earned a sabbatical and spent it on a month at Holden Village, a Lutheran retreat center located in the remote Cascade Mountains of Washington. Accessible only by boat, Holden is a place apart from phones, the internet, and technology. Soaring snow covered peaks surround this former copper mining village in the deep forest, a magnificent sanctuary for the hundreds of people who visit each summer. I was not sure what to expect of my month there. My plan was to read and rest, worship, and pray.

I had reached what I thought was a crossroads in my work and was unsure where to lead the congregation next, or if I should even stay in Danville. My glass-half-full outlook on life had been drained to what felt like an inch from the bottom of the glass. The aforementioned snarky people and hate mailer had led to my fantasizing about retirement bliss, and I was only forty-six! The strain of addressing Lynn's deep torment had cloaked Dave and me in melancholy. Additionally, Mr. D's existence had come to light. Dave had had a panic attack that made him realize he was messed up and his doctor finally diagnosed depression. Prozac helped him at first and then stopped helping him. Another med helped him, and then stopped helping him. My husband was back and then he was gone. He was often emotionally unavailable or a detached and brewing tempest. I needed a break from it all, which is what a sabbatical is meant to be. Holden Village would hopefully be the place for a recharge.

In my first week or so at Holden I read and slept, read and slept throughout the days. Surprised at how many naps I was taking each day, I came to the conclusion that my body was signaling my mind and spirit to just let down the burdens I chose to carry. Soon enough the need for so much sleep subsided and I began to immerse myself in creative endeavors. I attended classes, learning to weave, and tie-dyed shirts. I hiked to striking waterfalls. It was also freeing for me to not be in charge of a damn thing. I could just *be.*

My favorite class was "Queer Theology in the Year 2000" taught by a gay pastor. How could I resist attending a class with a title like that? I was disarmed by the progressive, open-minded spirituality of my classmates. Parents spoke about what they would do to help their own children to understand homosexuality. If their kids were gay, they wanted them to know that as their parents they would still love them, thus hopefully avoiding adding to the homosexual teen suicide statistics. *Jesus would love it here. They ask deep questions about God and are content to not always have answers. They are like me.* It was blissfully appealing. Holden felt like "Home," and my spirit was filled with serenity. My heart and soul united. Pretend Margie was nowhere to be found.

On a lovely August day, I settled in at my desk at Trinity, my first day back since my sabbatical. Sunshine streamed through the window of my office. All was peaceful. I was happy. It lasted not a day.

Soothed by a cup of tea, I began to tackle the stacks of papers in front of me, feeling more confident in the future than I had in quite some time. The sabbatical had convinced me I could stay at Trinity for an indeterminate period. Curiously, on the center of my desk was a manila file folder with a sticky note. "Thought you'd like to see these. Interesting!" It was signed by a dear-hearted woman from the congregation. Inside were clippings from the local newspaper, each one was a letter to the editor in response to a letter my Lutheran clergy colleague, John, and I had had published in that same paper on July 4, 2000, just before I had left for Holden. Our letter had been a response to a column written by a local conservative writer. We wrote:

> "On June 7, a local columnist wrote in support of
> Dr. Laura, a radio host who calls homosexuality

> "deviant."...That column implied that all Christians are of one mind regarding the issues of homosexuality. In fact, that is not the case..." We then wrote of a Lutheran bishop's reversal from condemnation to acceptance due to his experience with his gay son...who, as a teenager, prayed daily, in great anguish, that God would change him into a heterosexual man. The bishop realized that God did not change his son because God did not need to change him. God loved him and accepted him as he was. *Why is homosexuality such a threat that it calls forth so much hate among Christians? That is an important question to ask and wrestle with. We believe the issue of homosexuality is one of the pivotal ethical issues of the church in the 21st century. We also believe it is always better to fall on the side of grace, rather than law."*

John and I were pleased with our letter, feeling we had accomplished our intent and lent a fresh voice on the issue. Cut off from communication while at Holden Village, I'd had no knowledge of the firestorm of rhetoric that our letter had engendered back home. I was amazed as I flipped though the many letters. One pastor wrote a lengthy letter explaining that the Word of God contradicted John and me. It was nasty and derisive.

> "I can understand an atheist writing such a pro-sodomy-lifestyle piece. But it was written by two 'pastors,' a man of the cloth and (can we say?) 'woman of the cloth.' Now, let me say that in my heart I honestly love all men, these two people 'of the cloth' as well as all sodomites. How unfortunate that even people engaged in the most holy of professions cannot separate the issues of loving the sinner while hating their sin."

I wasn't surprised by his attitude, so I put my feet up on my desk, took another sip of tea and read on. Another gentleman said that we had fallen for the lie of the great deceiver, Satan, saying, "These two pastors should open their Bibles." He continued with scripture quotes to support his belief that homosexuality is sin. A woman wrote, "I believe that homosexuality is a sin punishable by eternal damnation." A gentleman named Drew sent me a handwritten letter advising me that homosexuality was a person's choice and that he would pray for my soul. "You are leading many down the wrong path, the path that leads to HELL!"

As I read through them I was truly not upset, but bemused by the hubbub our letter had caused. *Wow, this is something. I never expected this.* Not all was condemnation, however. Nine individuals had written to support us or to speak out against homophobia. A stand-out was, "I keep reading the letters to the editor and see the outright hatred from certain Christians. You can hide behind Bible quotes, but your hatred shows through." A lesbian named Wendy began her letter in this way. "To be applauded is the recent letter to the editor co-authored by Lutheran pastors John and Marjorie concerning the dignity and humanity of gay men and lesbians."

Wade was a letter writer who quoted from a message that had been bouncing around the internet which I had thought so clever:

1. I would like to sell my daughter into slavery, as stated in Exodus 21:7. How do I go about doing this? And what would a fair market value be?

2. I know that I am allowed no contact with a woman, or anything she has touched, while she is in her period of menstrual uncleanliness (Leviticus 15:19-24). Is there a way of telling when this period is occurring in a woman? Most take offense at such a question.

3. In Leviticus 25:44 it states that I may buy slaves from the nations that are around us. What if Mexico and Canada are not agreeable to this?

4. In Exodus 35:2 it states that one who works on the Sabbath should be put to death. Am I morally obligated to put them to death?

I laughed at this kindred spirit. Indeed, it had been an interesting read so far. Feet still up on my desk, I paged to the final letter to the editor in the stack. The newspaper had actually given the letter its own headline, "Pastors Don't Speak for All Lutherans." I planted my feet on the floor as a whoosh of nausea coursed through me. My heart rate rose. The authors were four of my local Lutheran clergy colleagues. It was a long letter since it took them many words to condemn us. We had made a "novel departure from the genuine Christian faith." Obviously, our colleagues disagreed with John and me, but that it was to the point of accusing us of "making God the author of sin," astonished me. This was an accusation of heresy. I was stupefied. Did our collegial relationship mean nothing? I immediately called John. "What a welcome back this is. I can't believe this."

"Neither could I, Margie."

"Did any of them call you before this was in the paper, you know, to discuss it first?"

"Not a word." John was particularly perplexed as one of the signers had lunch with him every week; another had been a seminary classmate of mine. We felt bamboozled. Blindsided.

The unconditionally accepting community of Holden had been like my seminary twenty years earlier. To come home to those pastors shafting me in that way was beyond heartbreaking. I didn't know the extent of its effect on me until later that day when I was sitting in the dentist's chair and he told me bad news about my teeth. I was facing a root canal and if that didn't work, extraction. More teeth problems. Really? I began not just to cry, but sob, and was really embarrassed. The dentist and his assistant tried to reassure me.

"But I'm not really crying about my teeth," I blubbered, "Although I'm not happy about this at all. I got betrayed by my colleagues today and this teeth news just comes on an already bad day." They left the room likely shaking their heads at this nutcase.

In the following days I walked around in a haze of despondency, feeling an affinity with Jesus when Judas, his friend, turned him over to the temple police. For collegial support, I now had no one but John. For an already lonely pastor to lose this group was titanic. Worse yet, Mr. D used this as an opportunity to pounce on me, delighted to have a new victim. The spiritual peace of my sabbatical seemed a dream, replaced with subconscious graffiti on my mind's wall. *You cannot trust your colleagues. You can't trust church members not to hurt you. Therefore, you cannot trust God either.* A bright spot was that the people of Trinity stood by me and were glad that our congregation welcomed "all" God's people. Nevertheless, this ugliness took on a dark energy and became the cornerstone block in that future hospital visitor's room, abiding there, waiting.

Eight years later in 2008, four years after we had left Pennsylvania for Florida, my denomination, the Evangelical Lutheran Church in America, voted at a national assembly to allow the blessing of gay unions and, as a consequence, to allow people in same-sex relationships to be ordained. "It's sin! The church has made a wrong turn!" was the protest. "It's about time. Thank God," said others. I wonder about my colleagues who had condemned me, and whether they were among pastors and congregations who then ceased affiliation with the ELCA. As for me, by the time of that decision, I was happy, but weary of the whole issue and would have been glad to head out of Dodge and be done with such church politics. "What do you think about this sexuality issue, Pastor?" I was asked one day as I stood at the church entryway in Wellington surrounded by a small group of people.

"I think God has more important things to do than worry about than who is sleeping with whom. This whole dispute keeps the Church from focusing on the important issues of feeding the hungry, helping the poor, and working for justice as Jesus told us to do." I was glad to see their heads nod in agreement.

Despite the deep scars I bear from the people who have tried to coax, change, or upbraid me regarding my liberality on sexuality, I know that their effort had the opposite effect from the one intended. It has led me to become even more of a champion for all marginalized citizens. I really like that about myself.

~

Undoubtedly, my years in Danville didn't provide me with the Home I desired, but thanks to two fine doctors, it did favor me with the unexpected benefit of ending the self-image problems I had continued to have due to my teeth. I tried not to let their appearance bother me and didn't think about them on a daily basis. Through the years I would lecture myself on my vanity. *Now come on, Marjorie, you are blessed in many ways. This should not be bothering you. Think of the black South Africans you met who had their shacks bulldozed by the government. Or the parents at the hospital with sick children. Teeth are not that big a deal. Really.* I wish I could say it worked but I carried in myself a sorrow that I kept hidden.

The orthodontist from my junior high school years had left two baby teeth in my upper row of teeth, to fill in the spaces of the missing ones that had never grown in. I became concerned that those baby teeth, meant to last maybe eight years in life, were loosening. They were now into their fourth decade so I had asked my dentists through the years, "What am I going to do about these baby teeth?"

Their answers were always passive. "Let's wait and see. We'll cross that bridge when we come to it." They were the experts. What did I know, other than anticipating how much worse I would look if indeed they were to fall out?

Our family dentist in Danville, however, chose to be proactive regarding my concern. He sent me to an oral surgeon for evaluation at the local medical center. Dr. Lessin was a gentle man, a manner all hope for in a doctor, and kind and caring. He examined me, stood back and said, "You have a very rich mouth."

"Tell me about it. Anything you can do? I'm really concerned about those baby teeth."

"Me, too. They're not gonna last." That simple admission made me like him: finally a man who tells the truth, no pussy-footing around. He took impressions of my teeth. "I'm going to assess this and get back to you." In my follow-up appointment, he and orthodontist, Dr. Seebold, a handsome, thirty-something fellow, offered me what they called their

"Tahiti plan" for my mouth. Dr. Seebold smiled as he explained, "It'll take awhile to get there, but the result will be paradise. Here's what we can offer you: Dr. Lessin will extract the baby teeth. Then I'll put on braces to move the eyeteeth over to where they should be. I'll also move your front teeth forward into a more normal position."

Dr. Lessin continued, "Then, I'll do jaw surgery to move your lower jaw forward to realign your bite. But since your chin is short—you really don't have much of a chin—we need to augment it, make it longer so that your face will look proportionate. Then you'll continue with the braces to get your teeth ready for bridge work on the top and bottom to fill in for the missing teeth."

"You're only forty, still young enough to reap the benefits," Dr. Seebold assured me, while Dr. Lessin nodded his head. "It is up to you, of course."

"Can I afford it?" I could. "How long will it take?" Three years. "Will I still be able to talk alright? I make my living public speaking, you know." Yes, my speech would be unaffected.

In addition to the discomfort of the surgery they told me it would be tough on my ego. I would be looking quite odd during the months when the eyeteeth were shifting, having large gaps in my upper tooth line. Dr. Seebold assured me that once there was enough space, he would insert fake teeth on the wire of the braces to fill in the gaps and make it look like I had teeth there. "Your Tahiti plan doesn't sound like a vacation to me." I lamented. Nevertheless, hope washed over me. "If it all leads to me looking more normal, I can put up with it."

And I did. All told, the entire process took four years. The surgery, one and a half years in, was successful. It was not without pain, and a memorably awful night post-op with nausea and vomiting. You know it's bad if you kick your husband out of the room, which is what I did. "Go home," I whispered, and then threw up again. Dr. Lessin did a marvelous job and there were no scars, little swelling, no bruising, and my jaws didn't need to be wired shut. I couldn't open my mouth very far for a few weeks, but over time and with exercise to stretch the jaw muscles, I was able to eat normally again. The colossal adjustment was in how I looked to myself.

I had left the hospital with a pressure bandage over my jaws and chin to keep the swelling down. It was Jacob Marley-esque without the knot tied on top of my head. I returned to the hospital three days later to have it removed. Dr. Lessin and his surgical resident hovered over the dentist's chair on which I lay and took off that bandage. Their faces brightened as they agreed with each other. "That chin turned out really well."

Then they handed me a mirror. Who was that stranger looking at me? I was more than astonished. In fact, I was stunned. My chin was way too long. I was certain of it. "I sure look different," was all I said, keeping my stupefaction to myself. What could they do? The deed was done. My mother, visiting to assist in my recuperation, was at my house when I returned. "Mom, look at me. I can't believe what they did. I look like I'm all chin. What am I gonna do?"

"It's really not that bad. It'll just take some getting used to. You look different, but it'll be fine. Dad would have said the same thing." I actually got a tape measure to see how many inches there were from the bottom of my mother's chin to her lower lip. Then I measured my own. The same. How can that be? "See," she said, "They made it okay. Just give it time."

"Oh, man. How do I get used to looking like this?" I called my husband at his work and declared, "Dave, I look like Jay Leno!"

When he returned home, he looked at my new face, gently kissed me so as not to hurt me, and declared, "You look good. It's different, but we'll get used to it." As I snuggled my head against his chest, a tear wet his shirt.

Dave and I did get used to it, but it took months. (Lynn reacted not to my face change but to my initial pain, which to me was not so bad, while Angela, at age six, was fairly oblivious to any change.) On approaching the bathroom mirror each day, I would repeatedly be surprised by the face looking back at me. Until the day—one I cannot pinpoint—when I wasn't. I was just me. I look at my post-op photographs now and wonder why I was so distressed. I look fine, just like mom had said. Perception, especially of change, is fickle and subjective. When, two years later, the braces were removed and the upper and lower bridges attached, it was with a gladsome heart that I viewed the person in the mirror—one who had normal teeth. My smile was now totally natural. I was a new person, not just in the way I looked, but as the transformation took hold in my life, in who I was inside.

A central tenant of Christian faith is resurrection, usually understood, in error, as only life after death. Christians who market Jesus as the way to avoid hell perpetuate this misconception. Resurrection is meant to be a this-life experience too, gracefully offering people a path to transformation and renewal. I have seen it in alcoholics who stop drinking, as sobriety is new life. This-life resurrection can be described as a salvation.

It's is a wonder when I get to witness it, which I have several times. With Ann, it began in her living room following a simple meal of Caesar salad and fruit. That afternoon my purpose in being there was to get better acquainted with her and to tell her more about Trinity Church. She was a dark-haired, petite, middle-aged woman with a live-in boyfriend at the time, and she told me of the trouble she had had dealing with her last two pastors. She had been part of two extremely conservative congregations, with more rules for behavior than I had ever known existed in any church.

"Since I've been coming to Trinity, I have to tell you it's very different. I like it. You don't make me feel bad about myself like my last two churches did."

"It certainly seems as if there were lots of rules to obey, from what you've told me." I said.

"There sure were. I told you that I'm divorced, but I didn't tell you that I've been married twice."

"That's rough on a person."

"It is, but I got conflicting advice from these pastors about what I was to do about it. I'm hoping you can help me, Pastor."

"What do you mean?"

"I went to one, and then the other, for what I thought would be counseling. My most recent divorce really had me down. I felt like such a failure." She paused as her eyes flooded. "I still do." I waited. "Well, anyway, the first man, who'd been my pastor for six years, told me that in the eyes of God I was still really married to my first husband since we're both Christians…and that my second marriage was not valid in God's eyes and I'd just been living in sin, and that I needed to go back to my first husband."

She saw my eyes grow wide as I shook my head. When I started to speak she said, "Wait, Pastor, there's more. I was mortified and confused, so I went to my current pastor at that time, the one before you. I was hoping he would help me. Well, he said that the other pastor was wrong, that I was still married in God's eyes to my second husband."

"Oh yeah, how so? How did he explain that?"

"He said that according to the Bible, I hadn't really been saved when I was with my first husband, that it wasn't a Christian marriage, that I was really still married to my second husband, and that that was the Christian marriage. He said I should go back to him. When I told him that was impossible, that he'd remarried, he told me I just had to live the rest of my life without a man, or I'd be committing adultery."

"Oh, Ann, I'm so sorry."

"But here I am living with a man anyway. I guess I'm a terrible sinner, but I don't want to risk another failed marriage. Tell me what you think, Pastor."

I sat quietly for a minute to collect my thoughts, knowing

my response would be important. "You know, Ann, the older I get, the more I figure we just muddle along in life, do the best we can, and God walks with us along the way."

She began to cry. Tears of relief? I guess I had said the right thing. Resurrection came to her in that moment and she was "saved," saved from the terrible law and judgment that had plagued her. God's love surrounded her, simply because I did not judge. I'd been an agent for grace. Ann joined the congregation and I saw her blossom as her "salvation" led her to become a natural in reaching out to newcomers. Grace became her guiding force.

Despite the God issues I have described and my slide toward unfaith, grace has kept me going and enabled me to keep doing my job. Grace, this-life resurrection, and transformation change people's lives, offering hope, peace, direction, forgiveness, and purpose.

My new face gave me resurrection. It certainly may seem petty and vain compared to Ann's travails or an addict's transformation, but it changed my life. I became more confident in my ministry. I learned to stand up straight, look people in the eye and smile readily. Never again did I hear the critique, "You need to smile more, Pastor." I look in the mirror now and smile, and am happy with what I see. I don't take that for granted. It's a new life, every day.

Devouring Myself, Losing God, Finding God

Hummingbirds, blue jays, cardinals, painted buntings, and doves are regular visitors at the bird feeders that hang from a post outside the large window looking into our Florida backyard. It's my secret garden, private and made beautiful by the butterfly-luring flowers and shrubbery I've planted. David hangs suet near the feeders as a special treat for the jays and woodpeckers. The birds get their foothold on the wire that surrounds the suet and then dig and peck and nibble at the fatty seed cake. The suet soon enough gives its life to nourish the birds.

Baseball players Chico Escuela and Sammy Sosa were known for saying, "Baseball has been berry, berry good to me." Well, Florida has been very, very good to me.

After my clergy colleagues threw me under the bus, I knew

it was time to leave that area. With no non-church friends, I had been lonely, but at least I had had my fellow pastors who understood the road we walked as church leaders. Without them, I was even more impoverished in spirit. Dave agreed that it was time to move. The shock of his Parkinson's diagnosis from a neurologist in Danville had just rocked us, so when I began yet another job search in late 2001, we knew it was only a matter of time until he could no longer work. It was, therefore, important for me to find a satisfying congregation for the long-term. My bishop assisted me in sending out applications to other bishops, seeking a congregation that could use my gifts. He said, "This won't take long. Good pastors never have problems finding a call. I'll write you an excellent letter of reference and you'll be on your way before you know it."

It took over two years of interviews and rejections: a long time. It was frustrating and particularly hard on young teenager, Angela. She knew I was looking, could not tell anyone, and never thought it would really happen since she saw me head off to interviews many times, and each time, come back empty-handed. Lynn lived around two hours from us with her young family and did not relish our relocating, but accepted it as necessary. My bishop was surprised that his prediction had been wrong. He surmised that my gender was a detracting factor and that as a pastor of twenty years experience I was less attractive on the congregational budget. If they had to pay someone more, they wanted it to be a man. I think he was right.

Finally, in June 2004, two and a half years after I began the search, I was called to serve the congregation of St. Michael

Lutheran Church of Wellington, Florida. As in the interview process for Trinity, I was chosen over a man despite the declaration from a gentleman on the interview team, "No way do I want a woman pastor." He met me, liked what I had to offer (Although at first he thought I was too thin for the job. Why are woman evaluated so much on appearance?) and then ceased any objection based on gender. "You were by the far the best candidate, so I eat my words."

I did not take this job because "someone finally wanted me." It had been too long of a wait for a new placement, with far too many rejection letters…I truly believed I could do good work there. Dave and I were excited, Angela less so. Leaving her childhood home and friends was to be challenging, so my mother's heart ached for her. And so, it was with mixed emotions that we decided to accept the offer.

Dave and I noticed immediately that people, in general, were much friendlier than they had been in Pennsylvania. Wellington is a classy, forty-year-old community, inclusive of diverse ethnicities. The village offers its residents beatific lakes, recreation fields, parks, and zones set aside for horses and equestrian events. Wonderfully, the forty-five minute drive from Danville to get to a decent store was now a five minute drive to a major mall. Of course, no snow to shovel or cold to seize up muscles are a great benefit to a man with PD. Additionally, West Palm Beach, twelve miles to the east of Wellington, offered us beaches, theater, and an airport.

People in the congregation brought a broader outlook to "doing church," since the majority of them were transplants, having lived someplace else before. (It is rare to meet native Floridians and when I do, I shake their hands for good luck like they're Bert, the chimney sweep in *Mary Poppins*.) For a congregation, varied backgrounds mean people have been exposed to differing ways of worship, music, church activities, and decision making. Hence, St. Michael was open to variety, creative ideas, and most of all, change. "Is your new congregation all old people?" was a question I heard more than once from Pennsylvanians when they heard the news that I was moving. To the contrary, St. Michael's congregation had a wide mix of adults, children, teens, and the stereotypical Florida retiree was a surprisingly low percentage of it.

I love Florida. I developed friends outside the church for the first time in thirty years, through my writing group. We met during the day so I could fit it into my odd schedule which had never been possible for me before with any non-church activity. This was really big. David has good medical care, providing him with the life-enhancing DBS surgeries. The weather affords me the ability to relax regularly on our backyard patio and to exercise via my daily walks. Lynn's two children, Alexis and Michael, think their "Florida Nana and Grandpa" are enticing and enjoy their visits from Pennsylvania to our area. Angela never took to life in Florida as well as her parents but she now assesses that time in this way: "I got to know people from different cultures, ethnicities, and lifestyles by living in Palm Beach County. My life in Danville seems so quaint in comparison."

I also really liked the congregation and felt gratified in

our partnership as pastor and people. Lots of people joined, drawn by my preaching—my prime ministry talent—and the grace-filled atmosphere that it engendered in the church. The atmosphere was primarily one of positive energy. Most of the congregation dove into many service projects and community activities. "What a gift you are to us, Pastor…I'm so glad my girls get to be part of this kind of church …No male pastor was able to get this new building built, but you did…Your sermons are some of the best I have ever heard. What a good storyteller you are. The messages are good for my faith…Your counseling helped me so much…You are amazing at what you do!" The praise was wonderful balm for my soul.

But. Yet. Nevertheless. Despite it all…

Over the years, I had felt smug when I heard of other pastors who, when overworked and unappreciated, had descended into flaming burnout. Not me. I had good self-care. I made sure I took my day off every week. Certainly, I continued to be more than frustrated at how often I needed to eat crow, that was not mine to eat, in order to keep peace in the parish. But I thought it was the right thing to do. I was often finding myself being big-hearted and sacrificial as a pastor is called to be.

However, the crow I had eaten for thirty years—rotten pieces of anger, bits of frustration, tidbits of sadness (for my isolation)—festered in my stomach. I was the bird *and* the suet. I was eating myself.

I have come to realize that when I lost God in the Cinder Block Room that day in August 2009, I lost a theistic God. What's that? It is God seen as a ruling entity "out there" and separate from the world. The classic characteristics of a theistic God are: all powerful, all seeing, all knowing, and unchanging. I certainly had evolved beyond the "classic" believer in all those traits of God. For example, when it comes to suffering, I have always been willing to toss out the characteristic of omnipotent in favor of an all-loving God, because I can accept the scholarly argument that since evil and suffering do occur, God could not be both all-powerful and all-loving at the same time. But who knows?

Nonetheless, before the Cinder Block Room, I had perceived God as a ruling creator who embodied love and therefore cared about me. I was known to God, and seen as God's special child. God made me as one of a kind and thought I was great. That was the God I lost that day. I missed him/her very much.

My thoughts after the Cinder Block Room showed this change in perspective. *No theistic God? I must be an atheist.* This was not a welcome conclusion. I've come to understand I really had became an agnostic, one unsure about God, but still willing to ask questions. Theologian Marjorie Hewitt Suchocki, author of *In God's Presence*, opines that "questions can be a way of drawing us into deeper realms of faith, taking us from belief in our beliefs to belief in the God who is more than our beliefs can express." Amidst my confusion and disquietude, I had to give up my belief in my beliefs and begin a reluctant new trek. Ever since the Cinder Block Room I had been on the hunt, following the scent toward my constant Friend.

In the beginning of this book I wrote about the party the congregation had for me for the thirtieth anniversary of my ordination. The people who attended teased me about my interest in the soap opera, *Days of Our Lives*, without knowing that only weeks before my days had mirrored that of a daytime drama. I had had an emotional breakdown.

How can you not like the ease of communication that e-mail and social media provides us? It's a great time-saver in parish administration. One of e-mail's big limitations, however, is not being able to see a person's face or hear their voice... which are often necessary when trying to comprehend or communicate well with another. Because one cannot see a person's face or hear their voice, an e-mail can easily be misunderstood. Additionally, folks can and do use the "perceived" anonymity of e-mail and online posting, to be downright horrid. Some have done it to me.

In April 2010, eight months post Cinder Block Room, I received another (in a years-long line) venomous e-mail from a member of St. Michael. "IS IT YOUR JOB AS A PASTOR TO RUIN PEOPLE'S LIVES?" My own anger spiked and I tried to keep my heart from racing. It was from a member who, from day one, seemed out to get me. Churchland has a name for such people: Alligators in the Parish. He certainly liked nipping at my ankles, always assuming I was deliberately keeping him from the leadership he desired in the congregation. In reality, it was the opposite. Understanding from people's feedback that his manner and demeanor often made them uncomfortable, I gave him job after job to try to find a workable niche for him wherein he could develop his strengths. In those duties, one after another, something went wrong and it was always "my fault."

I'd tried not to internalize the negativity. *He's a troubled soul. Folks can tell that. They see all you do to mitigate the problems he causes.* Three times, I had met with him at my office to stoically take yet another harangue. Those face-to-face attempts toward appeasement had gone for naught. I determined that I just had to put up with the abuse, which I did, silently, while continuing to be as kind and gracious to him as possible. My husband was the only one who knew the extent of it. My big mistake was shouldering the burden on my own instead of bringing in church leaders. "Never meet with such people alone" are the words that I should have obeyed. His recent e-mails had been particularly harsh and without the spiritual foundation I'd once had, I was more vulnerable to the attacks.

The e-mail above was strike one.

A month later, I was hit by strike two. A very active member of the congregation whom I liked very much, ended our pastor/parishioner relationship via e-mail with biting words and a cruelty that shocked me to my core. I had trusted her. She had told me, due to our heart-to-heart conversations, how close she felt to me. I thought she was my friend. Talk about blindsiding. Her rejection had been the worst sucker punch I'd received since the betrayal of my clergy colleagues ten years before. Truly shaken by her disdain and unwillingness to meet with me to discuss and reconcile, I got emotional when I told the Church Council of the loss of this pivotal church member, a leader in many activities.

"What happened?" they asked.

"I don't really know since she won't talk to me."

"We'll talk to her."

"Be my guest. Please try." She refused any contact with them, or me, and left the congregation. The child in me wanted to hide under a bed for a very long time.

Not two weeks later, another person whom I really liked, a good organizer and church worker in charge of a number of activities, got upset. He misunderstood something I'd said in an e-mail, got really mad and fired off a hostile message. I replied, trying to explain what I'd meant and apologized that I obviously had not worded it well. He fired off another, hotter message. I phoned: clearly, it was time to talk. I felt terrible that I had hurt him, especially someone whom I so admired. He refused my phone calls. I e-mailed him. He e-mailed back in an even nastier tone. I called again and left a pleading voicemail. I was flummoxed as to what to do, especially since he threw his responsibility for the upcoming Bible class, which was to begin in two days, on me. I'd been uninvolved in it and wouldn't know what to do to successfully lead it. He sent me a final, cut-off e-mail and then went silent. The whole situation was like none other I'd ever encountered. And you know I have encountered a lot. We later worked things out, but at that moment it was . . .

Strike three, you're out!

Panic permeated my at-home study like an entity. My heart pounded. I felt faint. Then I began to weep. I cried, and cried, and cried, and cried. Minutes, hours. An entire tissue box worth of tears and then some. I couldn't stop. The Cinder

Block Room had been a trifle compared to the abject despair and paralyzing fear that took hold of me and refused to let go. I tried to explain to Dave what had led to this and of course he didn't know what to do.

"What's wrong with me? Why can't I stop crying? I must be going crazy? Is this what it feels like to go crazy, Dave?"

"I don't know, Margie. I don't know."

I lay on our bed, sobbing. The caregiver became the one cared for as my husband lay spooning me, his arms around me. His sympathetic tears wet my back. Still, I cried. Dave shook with anger. "I'm so pissed off right now. I feel helpless. Look what the church has done to you!"

"I know, I know."

I got up and paced, hoping it would calm me. Nope, my weeping became shudders of breath. I fell to my knees and hugged a pillow from the sofa.

"Here's some tea. Maybe this will help you." It didn't. Hours went by during which time I tried a hot tub, a shower, TV, music, and a dark, quiet room. Afternoon became evening with my tears unabated.

"What day is it, Dave? I don't even know."

"Thursday."

"Thursday! How am I gonna finish my sermon for Sunday when I'm like this? There's something really wrong with me. I can't stop crying. How can I preach on Sunday? I'm a mess. I'm really scared for myself."

"Here, take this." Dave handed me a pill.

"What is it?"

"One of my leftover tranquilizers that I don't use anymore. Take it, get some sleep. You'll be better in the morning."

"You're probably right. It's like that crying jag I had during CPE when that boy died. Remember, I told you about it?" Dave nodded his head. "I'll be okay after some sleep."

I slept, but fitfully, awoke at 5:30am, and at once remembered the events from the day before. Tears immediately wet my pillow. *Maybe if I go for a walk. Those endorphins will make me feel better.* As the sun began to illumine the sky, my tissues and I began my usual twenty-minute walk around our neighborhood. I am a brisk walker, but not that day. An isolated car passed, but other than that, no one was out and about to witness my slow stride or my wet face. Images of injustices done to me flashed in my mind, amassing in an aggregate of blackness. The bowing palm trees and awakening bird calls provided me no solace.

Dave's right, look what being a pastor's done to me. I gotta finish a sermon today. Oh, who the hell cares? I can't do this anymore. What choice do I have? I have to work. Dave can't work. It's up to me. It's all up to me. Always, all up to me. You're all alone. What am I gonna do? Why can't I stop crying? You're really messed up, Marjorie, really, really messed up. You've wasted your life and for what? Christianity is bullshit! What a fool you've been.

Dave was waiting for me in the living room when I returned. "I was worried about you when I woke up and couldn't find you. Are you okay?"

"No, I'm not. I'm really, not. Still crying as you can see, can't stop for long."

"What do you wanna do?"

"I guess I have to find someone to preach for me and lead worship on Sunday because if I stay like this, I sure can't do it. And how can I finish a sermon or even care about it? I'll call when it's not so early and see if I can find someone."

"What can I do?" Dave's fear was apparent in his strained voice.

"Can you call Karen (the president of the Church Council) and tell her I can't be there this weekend? Let her know what's going on. She can handle things with the Music Director and others." He did.

Over the course of that morning, I continued to lapse into weeping with no ability to manage it. I was able to find a preacher to fill in for me. Karen stopped by and sat with me in my living room, listening to my rambling list of laments and watching me cry. She could obviously see my unraveling. She was a competent, caring leader so I knew I could count on her. "Take the week off, Margie. You need time to figure out what's going on. I'll take care of the details."

"Really?" I sniffed and rubbed my eyes.

"Yes, really. I'll even take care of that Bible class. I'll talk to him and make sure he still does it. It'll be fine."

"Don't tell him I'm having a meltdown or whatever the hell this is."

"You have a lot to think about. Take this time for you. The church'll be fine. You first, okay? I'll check in with you later. I'll tell everybody you're sick."

"And, I am, Karen, I really am."

And I was.

~

It is said that when we forgive, the main one who benefits is not the one forgiven, but the one who forgives. Forgiveness heals the heart.

I had once told a story in a sermon about a man who, over the course of a year, was treated for chronic pain in his neck and shoulders that was becoming debilitating, no matter the treatment: physical therapy, pain killers, creams. Nothing was able to touch the pain and ease the man's suffering. His doctor was frustrated, having run out of viable treatment options. Following his latest examination of the man and again finding no physical reason for his ailment, the doctor looked at him and said, "Who is it who is a pain in your neck?"

"My father!" his patient immediately blurted out.

Surprised at the quickness of the response, the doctor inquired further and learned of the perceived injustices from father to son, a sad tale indeed. "That's quite a story. It may be connected to your pain, actually. No standard treatment has helped you. I think you need to forgive your father."

"Never!" He stalked out of the office, obviously angry, and did not return.

Many months later an e-mail from that patient appeared in the doctor's inbox. Its one sentence said it all. "I have forgiven my father and my pain is gone."

On day three of my crash, crying still the order of the day, I went to my acupuncturist whom I had been seeing for a number of years to treat chronic pain across my shoulders. I figured a western medicine doctor would prescribe an antidepressant, which I knew might take a week or more to take effect. My fear for myself had sharpened and I needed something *immediately.* The doctor inserted hair-thin needles to boost my well-being while also burning moxa. "The moxa will release the negative energy around you," he quietly told me.

"What's that?"

"Dried mugwort."

"Really? I have no idea what that is but I'm open for anything if you think it'll help me."

I lay faceup on the table, listening to the soothing music, smelling the sage-like aroma while the tears streamed down to my ears. Thirty minutes later, I sensed the change, a difference in my spirit. I was still emotionally raw, but at least the perpetual weeping had ceased. The treatment opened me to a waveless space to breathe and think. The relief was palpable in Dave when he saw me come back into the waiting room. Now he was the one crying.

During that sick time off from work I visited a counselor whom I had seen in the past. I knew I needed to try to process what had occurred to me. Additionally, despite the June heat and humidity, I spent hours alone sitting in the backyard. I was consoled by the simplicity of the flowers, wildlife, and butterflies. A pileated woodpecker, the large Woody Woodpecker species, never before seen in our backyard, showed up and alighted in our mahogany tree. Was this beautiful bird a sign of hope?

When I returned to work I functioned relatively normally; the routine of daily activities that I'd been repeating for years enveloped me in a cocoon of familiarity. Everything seemed the same, but I was not the same.

Only a few people other than those in the Church Council knew what had happened to me. All who did showed me appropriate care and concern. What could I tell the congregation? "I went bonkers for awhile. I'm okay now." No, it was too early to speak of it since I wasn't sure what to say. I was not okay and found my fragility disconcerting and frightening. I had abundant internal work to do. Pretend Margie helped me get through that anniversary party only two weeks after my crash. I was glad for her.

A month later I took a weekend off in order to participate in a Radical Forgiveness weekend recommended to me by my counselor. The goal of the three days was to reframe *My Victim Story* so that it would no longer push my buttons or otherwise control me. I was skeptical, but hopeful. With floor pillows to support us, the five other lost souls and I sat in a room overlooking a backyard pond. The tranquil wooded area that we could see outdoors contrasted with the tension among us. *What's this weekend going to be like? Will it give me healing?*

First, I had to identify who had victimized me in order to move toward forgiveness. Two of the women, in their twenties and thirties respectively, had been sexually abused and so, of course, their victimizers had been their abusers. A forty-ish gentleman had had emotionally detached parents. One young woman was in danger of losing her husband due to unresolved issues she had with her parents. *Why am I here? Who is my victimizer? One of the e-mail writers? Or does it go back farther to Dave, Mr. D, and Parky? Or to the anonymous hate mail and my letter-writing clergy colleagues? Or much farther back to the engaged snake who dated me in seminary?* I certainly had numerous betrayers in my past, I realized.

Our first exercise was to take a white paper plate and draw a caricature face representative of our victimizer on it. Having participated in enough classes and retreats that used arts and crafts as a form of expression, I was game, but who was I to draw? I had to choose. I waited for inspiration, for something. Finally, in a childlike manner, I drew a two-faced visage, smiling and inviting on one side, sinister and menacing on the other. God. I drew God.

Mary, our counselor, instructed us to affix the plate to a tongue depressor stick so that it could be held up like a mask. "Get a partner and take turns holding up each other's plates in front of your own face. Then tell your victimizer what he or she has done to you. Tell them why you're upset and so messed up." We all looked at her with a you've-got-to-be-kidding expression. "I know it feels dumb and forced, but this is why you're here: to begin to get stuff out of you. Don't hold back. Take as much time as you need. Say the things that you've been holding in, things you've maybe never told anyone. This is a safe place here. We're in this together."

My partner went first and did a colorful, profanity-laced

job of calling her sexual abuser to the carpet. She yelled and cried as I held up her paper plate victimizer. I was moved by the intensity of her words, feeling real compassion for her for what she had endured as a little child. I wondered if choosing God as victimizer had been the right option for me. Surely, I had nothing even remotely parallel to say.

I took my place standing before the God-face held by my partner and haltingly, quietly began. "You know, God. I'm mad at you. Why did you ever call me into this job? That's why I'm angry, because you did. People treat me terribly. Christian people. I've been so lonely…years, no, decades of no friends, all because of being a pastor. Serving the church is supposed to be joyous. Well, it's not for me. Not anymore." I'd started out calmly but as I made my case against God the emotions welled up in me.

Counselor Mary came by to stir me up even more. She seemed to know that expressing our emotions would help us get all of the unspoken, rotting garbage out of our systems. "Tell God what you think. Tell him what he's done to you!"

My tears streamed, lapping at the corners of my mouth. I needed a tissue, but on I went. "You didn't let me know ministry was a sink or swim proposition. Nope, it's actually only sink sink, sink. Look what happened to me. I'm a mess. I'm afraid. I'm so afraid. I think I'm going crazy. I'm so tired of not being able to show how people hurt me. They continue to hurt me. I want to haul off and tell them how their petty issues with me and each other wear me down."

"Good, keep it up, get it out," Mary encouraged before walking on to another pair.

I continued my tearful barrage, my words taking on more fire. "They don't listen to me anyway since my sermons about grace and love don't get translated into practice. Why do I bother? Do I have to be their mother? I've had to eat so much stuff just to preserve the peace in my congregations and for what? I've done it at the expense of my soul. Who takes care of me? No one. Certainly not you. I hate you!" I was screaming.

Wow, did those words come from me? I hate God?

I've never been a yeller when it came to fighting with my husband, nor he to me, so this hollering was such a diversion from type for me. *Why didn't I bring any tissues?* I continued, "I have to hide myself, pretending things don't bother me. 'The Lord is my shepherd, I shall not want.' Bullshit. That is total bullshit! I have wants. Is it even worth having you in my life? I've wasted my freaking life for the church. I've wasted my life. You betrayed me."

There it was—the root of my problem. I felt betrayed by God. Up to that point I had no knowledge of that elephant in my life's room. That elephant finally had to knock me down so that I would listen. God's affectionate hand on my knee? Nope, God was beating me up. I was dumbfounded to discover that I saw God as my Judas.

The Talmud distinguishes between a robber and a thief: a robber will hold you up, face to face, and steal your property. A thief will ease into your life and, having won your confidence, slowly take all that you own. It seems I saw God as a thief who had stripped me of myself. The thief and I had a collaborator—Pretend Margie—whom I thought had gone away. She was actually alive and well. She had been conspiring with God to consume me.

As the weekend progressed I had other opportunities to name my pain, claim it, and then release it. Identifying the core negative beliefs that had driven *My Victim Story* was key to finally becoming healthy. The negative beliefs were there due to lies I had told myself. I had integrated them into my subconscious. My body felt the burden of them in the chronic pain across my shoulders and neck. I had believed the following lies:

- I will be betrayed, therefore I expect people to hurt me.
- I am all alone.
- I don't fit in.
- Grace is not returned to me—to pastors.
- No one takes care of me or defends me.

These lies had kept me a victim, leading to my perceived abandonment by God. The activities that followed invited each of us to more deeply understand how our *Victim Story* had overpowered us. Each of us shared our relevant histories so the group heard about my overachieving ways in elementary school and beyond. I told them about Mr. D and Parky, the trials of parenting Lynn during her rough years, and a number of the aforementioned betrayals about which I have already written. It was not a lovely walk down memory lane. It was more like carefully finding my way through a mine field. Nevertheless, it was such catharsis to get it all out. We even each had a turn whacking the hell out of a pillow with a tennis racket while we poured out all the dreck, replacing the negatives with positive statements and subsequent whacks. For instance, my wallop as I yelled my negative, "I am afraid," was countered with "I will not be afraid."

On the final day, after some further exercises calling each of us to see how our victimizer may have actually helped us become stronger, more enlightened persons, Mary guided us to the denouement of the retreat, the "Reframe."

"Okay, it's time to reframe your victim story and give thanks for the things it's taught you. I want you to write about what you've learned. Here's a paper with the opening words to use to get you started." I read the words that were meant to prompt me.

> "I now realize that what I was experiencing was a precise reflection of how I perceived the situation through the lens of my victim consciousness. I understand that I can change the original experience by changing my perception of it and am now willing to see it as having been a blessing in my life—an experience that leads to spiritual growth. I have now released my attachment to *My Victim Story.* I am at peace with it and here's how I see it now."

Give thanks for what it has taught me? Huh? I had ten minutes to write. Ten minutes! Surely that was not enough time. I had no idea what to write, truly. But the clock was ticking so I dived in. The words wrote themselves. I'd been inspired when writing sermons, but this was a flow like no other. I completed my reframe story in less than the allotted time. I knew it to be my truth. I had to learn to forgive myself and forgive God. Truth's seed was planted, but its growth would take time to root...perhaps the rest of my life. This is what I wrote:

> *I now realize that I thought God had really messed with my head. How? I felt alone and a misfit in my family, school, and in my body so much so that the only way I could try to feel whole was by getting good grades. Hence, I always tried to overachieve in life, work towards righteousness, and be better than the people who I felt made me feel alone and who did not pay attention to me.*
>
> *But then the fundamentalist Christians ("fundies"), to whom I linked myself for a few years in college, helped me see that I did not need to prove anything to God or myself—that God loved me as I was. But the fundies, being walking contradictions, loaded on the guilt and judgment in their religious self-righteousness. This turned my stomach and my soul knew it was not Love. I got the hell away from them and their dark ways.*

I now knew Grace and Love and planned to live that out as a pastor. Here is where God laughed. The darkness of needing to "achieve" acceptance and love kept returning to me in people who betrayed me so that I would not believe in the love that I knew. Pastors around me were such disappointments. I was one of the few who was not, I thought. Do you see that self-righteousness?

God laughed some more and led me to a man who tried my patience so much that I wished him dead on a regular basis. His depression and resulting unreliability made me work even harder to be strong and capable. Therefore my self-righteousness grew because of what I had to endure from Mr. D who lived in our house in my husband's body. He turned David into a walking zombie of unavailability. To top it off, after Mr. D finally left, Parky moved in to again make me the achiever who had to be strong. I felt even more alone.

Meanwhile, in Churchland, I conveyed and taught unconditional Grace and Love and made a big impact on many people. However, my soul kept drawing in fucking assholes who treated me like crap. Their ungrace-filled behavior led me to believe that grace did not work, that Love was powerless, that Love does not beget grace.

But they are wrong.

I am not alone. Grace does change people. No one needs to earn God's Love, especially not me. My purpose continues to be to show unconditional Grace and Love in my work and life. I will continue to speak out and tell people that religion is not so much about concern for sin as about healing brokenness. I will tell them that God does not send people to hell.

I will let God heal My Victim Story. I will let God love me. I will no longer feel that God betrayed me. God used my life experiences of betrayal and hurt as a contrast to the powerful grace the fundamentalists first showed me almost forty years ago. Grace can transform. The fundies could never truly accept it themselves, but I will. I will.

Two images come to mind as I assess how, over the decades, I moved from sprightly and cheerful to one awash in morbidity. Image number one comes from film. In *Star Wars Episode IV: A New Hope* the Force is described by Obi-Wan Kenobi as an energy field created by all living things, surrounding and penetrating living beings and binding the galaxy together. The characters rely on the positive Force to do feats of daring as well as acts of compassion. The Force's contrasting dark side feeds off emotions such as anger, jealousy, fear, and hate. Both sides of the force lay within both Luke Skywalker and Darth

Vader. The image is not unlike the Lutheran theological concept of being both saved and sinner at the same time. This is: we hold within ourselves the good and the bad, often sparring with each other.

Image number two is of a story in which an old Cherokee told his grandson, "My son, there is a battle between two wolves inside us all. One is evil. It is anger, jealousy, greed, resentment, inferiority, lies and ego. The other is good. It is joy, peace, love, hope, humility, kindness, empathy, and truth."

The boy thought about it, and asked, "Grandfather, which wolf wins?"

The old man quietly replied, "The one you feed."

The power of the negative, the dark side of the force, so to speak, was strong in *My Victim Story*. I'd been feeding it for years. "Margie," Dave would often say to me, "You've got a great memory but it really works against you. You remember all this negative stuff. Don't sweat the small stuff."

"Easier said than done. You really don't remember the yucky stuff that happens to you?" I would respond.

"Not like you do. You're cursed."

"I agree with you there. I wish I could forget it!"

Joe Dispenza in his book, *Evolve Your Brain*, explains that we essentially think our reality. Neurologically speaking, our thoughts create, as he puts it, hard-wired neural pathways that come to define us on a daily basis. Negative thoughts strengthen life-annulling neural pathways; positive thoughts boost the favorable, life-affirming pathways. When I would bring to my mind a negative event and seethe about it, I fed those chemical reactions into a pathway that made it easier for my brain to focus on the unfavorable experiences time after time. Dispenza avers that a person *creates* himself or herself, i.e. their world view. I had unconsciously created a world that slanted toward shadow and it had slowly been neutralizing my optimism and hope. Clearly, my overachiever could have gotten an "A" in negative thinking about church, God, and life.

Dispenza's solution is to rethink yourself. He calls it the science of changing your mind. *My Reframe Story* pointed me in the right direction to do that. I had to acknowledge what I already knew, that grace has the real power to transform my life. Ungrace was and is an illusionary power. Grace—unexpected, unmerited acceptance and love—is what had drawn me into ordained ministry. Heck, even Darth Vader turned to the light side of the Force eventually. *Can I think my way back to spiritual health?*

An important step in my healing has been to name the nullifying experiences out loud, thus beginning to expel them from my subconscious. Then when the memories arise I can, in full awareness, decide not to view them through my wounded myopia. Instead, as counselor Mary told me, "Then you can say, 'Oh, that's just *My Story,* coming up again. It has no power over me anymore.' Instead give thanks for what the experience taught you and how it contributed to the person you are now. Then, let it go."

I imagine a wooden bucket held together with metal straps. Perhaps I should call it my waste bucket, the place in which my brain stored the toxic events, large and small, that eventually contributed to my crash. Over the years there were drips as well as cupfuls of crap that began to fill my bucket. It became my individual Bucket of Despair. When I began to cry on Crash Day, the metal strapping of my bucket had given way and a tsunami flooded my soul. "Whoa, baby," my poor brain said, "that is a lot of shit heading this way all at once!" My brain's fight or flight response could no longer help me. It broke down. I broke down.

What was in that bucket? Inspired by that Radical Forgiveness weekend, I began writing this book to find out. In the writing, I have rummaged around in my memory in order to face the experiences that had lain in wait to jump out and attack me. I had recycled negative paradigms frequently. I highlight them below.

1. **The unexpected isolation and loneliness that has been mine as a pastor.**

The daytime drama, *Days of Our Lives*, has been an off-and-on guilty pleasure for me for thirty years. As "my couple," Patch and Kayla, had left the show around 1990, I hadn't watched it much. But they returned to the show in 2006 and watching became fun again. How could I resist the age-old soap opera story line of Steve "Patch" Johnson returning from the dead? There is dead dead, and then there is soap dead, after all. What added to the experience, and actually changed my life, was discovering the online community of Steve and Kayla fans. I began to write fan fiction. I had previously not written any fiction (or much else for that matter) beyond sermons and religious articles. I laughed every single day from some clever remark posted by one of my many online fan friends. We were all a bit obsessed and loved being that way.

I took my fandom to a new level and began to attend events where I could meet the actors who played Steve and Kayla, Stephen Nichols and Mary Beth Evans. One of these events had me flying solo to Los Angeles for a *Days of Our Lives* weekend. I had more fun than I had had in years, ogling the hunky actors, talking to women who had previously been just names on my computer screen, and delighting in being noted by Nichols and Evans as a pastor, one who brought them each fair trade coffee, too.

In Burbank one day, as I sat with a group in front of a Starbucks, my new fan friends were freely swearing in front of me. They all knew I was a pastor and it did not stop them. I was not offended. Instead, I was overjoyed. I was just one of them. *This is the first time since seminary thirty years ago that I can be myself.* What a paradoxically sad revelation that was... that I had lived with Pretend Margie dominating me.

2. **Frustration due to feeling that I cannot express my anger.**

A few years ago, I worked on a committee with a certain gentleman who was difficult to work with. He seemed to delight in being a contrarian, but since he was a "pillar of the congregation," I did not want to stir up trouble by confronting him. I knew he might talk to his wife and his friends about it and that that might spread to their circles in the congregation and beyond. "Don't borrow trouble" came to mind as well as my concern about not harming his faith, so I patiently put up with him. Unexpectedly, he stopped at my office one day, expressed his "love" for me, and then told me point-by-point how to be a better pastor. I wanted to smack him. I really did. Instead, I actually thanked him for his concerns and poured a spleenful of I-so-hate-my-job into my heretofore unknown brain's bucket.

3. **Managing a community is an unyielding challenge**.

Pastor Steven L. McKinley wrote a whimsical column about daily life in the parish in a now-defunct professional magazine called *Lutheran Partners*. As I identified with his following description of work life for a parish pastor, I laughed sadly when I read it.

> "One day Rabbit came to my office complaining about the unreasonableness of Otter, and when Rabbit was finished with Rabbit's lament about Otter, Rabbit moved on to the rudeness of Sparrow. And then I had a phone call from Bear that was mostly concerned with the shenanigans of Lion and why I was not being more direct in dealing with Lion…Pigeon called me to tell me that no one wanted to listen to what Pigeon had to say, how people ignored Pigeon and talked

> rudely to Pigeon. Turtle called me up to let me know that Muskrat was still unhappy about not having been given sufficient public recognition for a financial gift Muskrat had made…"

Pastor McKinley was so clever. I once used his words as in illustration of parish life in a sermon, following which a forty-something man approached me. "I enjoyed that description of the church people as animals. Does that kind of thing happen here?"

"Every week." I smiled as I saw his shocked expression.

"I wouldn't want your job," he said in commiseration.

"On many days, neither do I." He laughed and touched my shoulder with support.

Yeah, it's funny when you can step back from it, but the woodland creatures' sniping and snarling had darn near killed my optimism. I came to expect people to hurt me. I learned to mistrust first and ask questions later. My job became one I endured more often than I enjoyed.

The above three subtexts of my life had unfolded without my being aware of them. Thus, the dark Force became so strong in me. No wonder my brain's bucket of crap got deep. *Your mission, Marjorie Weiss, should you decide to accept it, is to come over to the light side of the Force. Salvation, in its true sense, is there. And hope. And God, whatever that now means to you.*

My experience with the Cinder Block Room changed me. Losing God, it seems, was necessary so that I would trek to this day. My emotional crash changed me, too. It was a purging necessary to integrate my mind, body, and spirit. It led to my own this-life resurrection.

November 2012

As I write this, it's been two years since my breakdown and three since the Cinder Block Room. I've been blessed with a peaceful sabbatical month in Berkeley, California. I am staying in a guest house at The Church Divinity School of the Pacific while writing, reading theology, and escaping into just-for-fun novels. It's time for me to face The Big God Question I have had to push to the recesses of consciousness. As I moved from one activity, sermon, or class to the next at work, there was little of me left to face it.

As I planned my sabbatical, I felt drawn to the description of this Episcopal seminary, with the hope that I could fill up spiritually. I go almost every day to daily worship, content to soak in the atmosphere, the music, and the words. Not being up front leading lets me focus on thinking about the God I seek instead of about what I need to do or say next.

Hence, I have been experiencing a different flow. It has surprised me. Initially, I got emotional during each worship service. Emptiness washed over me. I was afraid that I would always feel lost and cut off from a faith that had once sustained me. *How can I continue to be a pastor when my faith seems nil? Was I really this unaware of how spiritually bereft I've become?*

Even after everything I have learned and written? The answer seems to be, yes. Here, in this safe place, I have given myself permission to feel right down to my toes: the grief, the despair, the phoniness I have embodied. It has been hard work but necessary.

A song chanted at one of the worship services I attended, touched me deeply. "I am the God that healeth thee, I am your God, your healer. I sent my word and healed your disease, I am your God, your healer."

Can I be healed? Julian of Norwich, a fifteenth-century Christian mystic, also spoke to me across the centuries. "All shall be well, and all shall be well and all manner of thing shall be well." I translate this into: be at peace. Stop trying so hard. Let be.

"Dave," I said to my husband before leaving for California, "my plan is to finish my memoir when I'm out there, but I don't know what the end will be. I haven't lived it. I sure hope I can come up with something." Imperceptibly, it has happened. Healing has happened. An ending and a new beginning. Despair at worship has changed to feelings of gratitude and shalom. Happy tears now can wet my eyes.

Shalom, often translated as "peace," is more than that. It is wholeness and harmony with self and the world. My spirit has begun to reverberate with shalom. It is as though I have been dunking my head under water for a long time and have finally come up for air. My breathing is fresh and new. Rebirth. What did it? It's a mystery. My best guess? Time apart, attention to my inner world, and concentration on my needs rather than the needs of others. I am certain that my choice to be here in a loving seminary community has given me renewal. Some students have adopted me. We eat together and I ask them about their studies. They are eager to hear about my years of experience in ministry. It has taken me back to the warm fuzziness of my own seminary days. I've also had conversations on deep God issues with three caring professors. Their genuine concern for me as I told each about my "dark nights of the soul" has been heartening.

Finally, perhaps most importantly, observing these students who are preparing to jump feet first into ordained parish ministry has been invigorating. They are really striving to live and learn faith. It's inspiring. They lift me up just by their everyday connection with the divine. Love is in this place, among these students and staff. I am stunned and gobsmacked by the change this month has brought in me. God has shown up! I am so over-the-moon happy about it that I cannot truly convey the relief that I feel. I cried in joyous relief about it one evening as I roamed the first floor of the guest house of which I was the only occupant at that time. I felt enveloped by a Presence.

There is much I still do not know about myself, but the following statements are what I now want to embody, model, and live by.

1. I am at peace to not know all the things of God. This is a big deal for me: to be comfortable with mystery.

2. Love is my Ground of Being. The letter of First John in the New Testament says simply, "God is love." God's light and love have been within me unceasingly, but each got pushed aside and minimized by my brain's ever-filling waste bucket. God can now be a metaphor for the personification of Love. Love has energy and power and the sparkle of affirming life. Is God a being? I doubt it. Is God, Being? I think so. I don't know if I will ever find a metaphor that will explain to my satisfaction the abstractness of God as Being. The best I can say is that God-is-love energy connects all people and all things. Therefore, God is within, already there, always present, and always involved.

3. It is not my job to figure out God and faith or to make them rational. I am arrogant to think that I could. People have struggled with the concept of God since evolution moved *Homo sapiens* into consciousness. How can anyone understand God when God is bigger than our words, our brains, our worldviews, and our imaginations?

In his book *Velvet Elvis,* Rob Bell refers to Moses' call from God. Moses is skeptical and asks, "And who shall I say is calling?" God replies, "I Am." As Bell writes, "That doesn't really clear things up, does it?"[3] Moses is looking for a god he can wrap his head around, a god that makes sense. "I Am" implies mystery. Bell says that perhaps this is God's way of communicating. "If your goal is to figure me out and totally understand me, it's not going to happen. Even my name is more than you can comprehend."[4]

As the story in the Bible goes, the day Moses learned God's name was when he was before a fiery bush that did not get consumed. Astonished and in awe, Moses took off his shoes because he knew he was on holy ground. Later, when Moses asked for reassurance that God was really there, he desired something tangible—just as I did on those late, anguished nights on my living room sofa. For the tangible, God allowed Moses to see God's back after passing by. Not much, huh?

Yet, Bell says rabbis have argued that in the original Hebrew language the word "back" could be understood as a euphemism for "where I just was." Rob Bell agreed when he wrote that it is as if God is saying, "The best you're going to do, the most you are capable of, is seeing where I just was."[5]

Seeing where God-is-love "just was" in my life is to be my ongoing quest. I imagine a new bucket in my brain, the place to put holy experiences—the God moments. Or perhaps a better image might be that of a stream with many tributaries, flowing through my subconscious, permeating into all the anterooms and cubbyholes of my being and filling me. It is important to continually bring those moments to my conscious mind so that I may be directed by the power of God-is-love rather than that bucket full of nullifying waste. Where is the holy ground on which I have walked? Where have been my ordinary moments that got filled with something else? Where are the places where God just was?

My sister, Susie, and I zip down a snowy hill on a cold winter's day. We're innocent, fearless children. She is on her belly on the sled; I lay atop her on my belly. We hit some gravel. The sled and Susie stop dead. I go flying, landing facedown in the gravel and ice. Blood runs from a cut above my right eye. When I arrive home, crying from the fright of it all, my mother patches me up. She then takes me into her arms and rocks me by the warming radiator. It will become the only childhood memory, other than the car ride to the hospital after I was hit by the car, that I have of my mother snuggling with me. I cherish it. Holy Ground. God-is-love.

At the worship service when I was being ordained, the bishop and other pastors had just laid their hands on me as a symbol of God's Spirit coming to me in a special way. More special to me, however, were the hands of my father after the service as he hugged me and whispered in my ear, "I love you." I always knew he loved me. This was the first time in many a year that he had said it to me out loud. Holy Ground. God-is-love.

After giving birth to Angela, I lay in the hospital bed observing eleven-year-old Lynn seeing the new baby for the first time. I remembered how often during the pregnancy she had told me how much she hated me and the baby. Dave and I knew she felt threatened and afraid. Dave placed the swaddled infant in her arms. She looked at the baby in awe and then at me. "I love her, Mom." Holy Ground. God-is-love.

~

Dave, Angela and I were on vacation at a secluded beach in Virginia. In a dune near a concrete sea wall, I found a large conch shell, complete and whole. "Here's another one," nine-year-old Angela said with delight. "And another one!" The glorious sunshine suddenly hid behind ominous dark clouds that had come at us with a rush. Dave reluctantly ran to gather our things as I tried to coax Angela away from the dune. Her long, blond, curly hair was billowing around her. She found two more conch shells. "Oh, Mommy, do we have to go?"

"It's going to rain, in fact, it just started!" I yelled, since the wind was whipping and sand had begun to graze our faces.

"But look, there're more shells," Angela said with yearning. The rain was washing away the sand, revealing a trove of shells. Dave gave up trying to get us to carry things to the car. Instead, he joined us as we pulled shell after shell from that dune. The wind was fierce, the rain stinging. Our laughter was louder than the gales as the three of us joined in the treasure hunt. Time stood still. We were one with nature. I will never forget it. Holy Ground. God-is-love.

~

When she was in her late twenties, our daughter, Lynn, found her birth father. Dave and I listened to her on speakerphone when she called us in Florida from her Pennsylvania home to tell us about her first phone call with him. She was over-the-moon and we were very happy to hear the news. "He has a picture of me on his living room wall from when I was really little. He was so excited to hear from me."

Dave's eyes welled up when he said, "This is nice to hear, Lynn. It must make you feel good to know he thought of you."

"It sure does. He used to visit me at the foster home, but once they adopted me, he couldn't come anymore. He didn't know the same family that fostered me had adopted me."

"I guess you told him that they kicked you out. What did he think about that?" I asked. "Especially since he obviously knew them?"

"He was not happy about that at all. It really upset him."

"What did you tell him about us?" I laughed when I said it and teased further. "Good things, of course, right?"

"I told him you were wonderful."

Dave and I both laughed loudly with a whoop and simultaneously said, "Yeah, yeah, so wonderful!" We were enjoying the family joke since we all knew how tough it had been.

Lynn did not say anything. There was silence on her end of the phone. Dave said, "Lynn, are you there?" We waited. "Lynn?" She was weeping.

She said with a tightened throat, "You guys were so wonderful to me, even when I was so awful. I told him I wouldn't be who I am without what you did for me." A three-way weep commenced.

The daughter who once declared to us, "Stay out of my life!" had said words we never thought we would hear. Holy Ground. God-is-love.

~

A few years later, Lynn graduated from college. She had attended classes, often with a full course load, while still working full-time. It was a big achievement so family members attended a celebration picnic afterward at my brother Steve's and his wife, Donna's, Pennsylvania backyard. Lynn was close to them. When Lynn had been a high school senior, her life at school and home, and our lives with her, had become incredibly tense. So she had moved in with Steve and Donna for what would become six months and in that time she had graduated (from the same high school Dave and I had attended in Oley). Hence, they had been surrogate parents to her.

The picnic was a grand occasion since Lynn had doggedly earned a business degree while working full-time and managing a busy family as wife and mother. Besides Lynn's husband and their daughter and son, those attending the picnic were Angela, Lynn's in-laws, assorted Weisses, and Lynn's birth father, George. Before the meal, we paused for a prayer. Steve, as host, prayed, "God we want to thank you for Lynn and her accomplishment. She's worked very hard, supported by her husband and kids. We also want to thank you that we have three sets of parents here to support her today. We all represent times and people in her life that have shaped her. Bless us now as we share this meal. Amen." A shiver coursed through me.

He was right, three sets of parents—Dave and me, Steve and Donna, and George. Holy Ground. God-is-love.

~

In May 2004 I led the final worship service as Pastor at Trinity Lutheran Church in Danville. I had begun my ministry there twelve years earlier on another May Sunday. It was fitting to end at the same season that had once been a beginning. There was a higher than normal attendance, the pews filled with smiling-sad faces. Goodbyes were bittersweet. About midway through a Lutheran service is the sermon. Since I am sometimes a crier in my goodbyes, I was pleased with myself that I delivered it without a tear.

The sanctuary of this 1870s-era building is old style, one I never liked. It has a long rectangular space with a center aisle, wooden pews that can seat 250, a front chancel with an altar and seats for the choir set apart and some distance from the pews. I dislike the perceived separation between pastor, the altar, and the people. I always felt remote from the congregation, having to stand or sit so far away.

Following the singing of a hymn, we received the offering. During the offering, I took my usual spot in the faraway chancel. It's up four steps, as far front as one can sit, in a large wooden throne-like chair. Two singers, Dave (not my Dave) and Amy, took their places at the microphone which was located down the steps, to the front and right of me, by about twenty feet. Dave announced a special surprise song they were to sing, a duet, in my honor. *How nice.* He turned to his left and looked over his shoulder to where I was sitting and said, "This is for you, for how we feel about you." They begin to sing, *You Raise Me Up*, a song made popular at that time by singer Josh Groban.

I liked the song and was immediately touched by the sentiment behind it. I sat on my perch so far from the people in attendance, listening and enjoying their voices.

The moment was so beautiful. I looked out on the congregation, seeing people I had known and loved for so many years. The harsher memories faded. As Dave and Amy's voices blended in harmony, I was "overtaken." There is no other word to describe it. I began to cry. No matter that I'd hoped to make it through the service without them, staying the tears was impossible. Tears ran down my face and onto my neck, my lip quivered. I looked to the worship assistant who sat near me, a banker in his early fifties. He was crying. I peered down at the congregation and watched as a wave, yes a wave, of sentiment and emotion swept through the pews. Looking back on that moment, I saw God-is-love spread pew by pew. Wet faces, red eyes, blowing noses, smiles. Tears of joy for who we had been together. Sadness. An ending. But not "the end" as we will always be connected in God. It is, as the song said, a glimpse of eternity.

Dave and Amy finished their song with a crescendo. The pianist finished the final notes. Silence. Holy silence. God was is in this place. God-is-love. Holy Ground.

I sat sometimes in Barnes and Noble with my writing group: Fran, Cheryl, Pat, Dawn, and Karen. The café is our regular meeting place. We poured over the submission for the day that one of us has written. Laughter permeated the cozy zone that had become Us. We drank our tea or lattes, nibbled at biscotti and cookies. I have friends. I am not alone. Holy Ground. God-is-love.

May I always remember these things.

~

Am I happy? On more days than before, yes.

Do I have peace? Not always, but I sense that my interconnectedness with all people and all things gives me a hopeful outlook on my path.

Do I understand God? Heck no, but I perceive more than I once did.

Do I still hate God? No, I thank God for all the experiences, painful and beautiful, that have formed me into the me of today. This gratitude has enabled me to feel forgiveness for the three people whose "strikes" triggered my breakdown and for others about whom I have written, even the poison pen writer. Jesus was right about the importance of forgiveness. Of course, he was!

~

EPILOGUE

The condensation drips on the outside of my empty gin and tonic glass. I gaze at the ice cubes inside that are dancing with the lime wedge as I put it down. "Well, God, I've enjoyed our drink together and our chat. Very enlightening. Thanks. I want to tell you something important." I pause, to collect my emotions so that I can say it. "I love you. I just got lost in toxicity. It made me blame you. I'm sorry. I also thank you."

"You're welcome. I'm always glad to see you or hear from you. I want to tell *you* something important." God pauses and tears well up in God's eyes. "I love you very much. I'll never leave you. That toxicity? That's what I call sin. It breaks a lot of people." She-He playfully kicks some sand onto my feet. "You know, you can be a lot of fun, a challenge, but exciting and interesting. I sure made you deep!"

"That you did." I muse, reluctant to rise. "My, we've talked a long time and the hot desert sun never bothered me once. Great oasis."

"Oasis? What Oasis? Look back, Margie. Look back."

"What?" I turn around expecting to see the many dunes through which I had trudged.

"Wow, wow, wow. Look at that!"

Before my eyes is a paradise of lushness and beauty. Trees of gold and red, a lake of iridescent blue, a meadow of wildflowers resplendent in colors I have never seen before. Butterflies, my favorite thing of pure joy, are in abundance. Beautiful, magnificent, heavenly.

I look at God, astonished. "I don't understand. How can this be? I came that way, I know. It was a desert." God laughs. "Mystery. I love a good mystery, don't you?"

AFTERWORD

September 2018

In the years that have intervened since I completed this book and have gotten it into print, things have happened. I am now retired and living a very content life in a Fifty-five-Plus community in St. Lucie County, Florida. This has been an excellent place for us to have built a home since its activities and clubs have given me an easy inroad into friendships. I am simply one of the gang and am happier than I could have imagined. I started a knitting and crocheting club and find my main passion in daily knitting. I have also been able to do things as a volunteer that often had called to me in the past, but for which I never had time. Being hostess at the surgical waiting room at the medical center is one. Sewing for the theater club, another. I took a class in conversational Spanish. I planted and maintain a butterfly garden in my effort to save Monarch butterflies from extinction. I've also had great fun singing in my community's musical theater. I do preach occasionally to fill in for a pastor on vacation. Yet I am very surprised that I do not miss being the Queen Bee.

I chose to retire earlier than sixty-six so that I could be more available to Dave and so that we'd have the leisure time to travel together and do other activities while he still can. We have been to Alaska, the Black Hills of South Dakota, the Maritime Provinces of Canada, and look forward to the national parks in Utah and a river cruise in Europe. We also take advantage of the local places to hike and observe the water birds.

On Dave's most recent visit to his neurologist to have his deep brain stimulation tweaked, the doctor observed him with great pleasure since he has had "a remarkable response to DBS." He's had twelve and ten years respectively with the implants and they are still helping him live a life that borders on normal. However, Parky took away his ability to drive, and also messes with his balance, his memory, and getting his feet to listen to where he wants them to go. PD also sometimes gives him wild nightmares during which he sometimes swats me! He also has become soft-spoken due to PD's effect on his breathing. I say "What?" or "Huh?", or "Pardon?", or "Say that again," often. (I had my hearing checked and it is not me.) Speech therapy has helped him I am happy to say. Yet Dave defies Parky and hops on his recumbent trike to go play pool or make fifteen-mile rides.

Lynn now has a Master's in Business Administration which has led to her having a satisfying job. Alexis and Michael are grown so she and her husband, Justin, are wondering how life will be for two forty-year-olds in their Pennsylvania empty nest. She continues to have a relationship with her birth father and assorted biological siblings and half siblings. She has read this book and has given me her permission to include her story in it.

Angela is making a life for herself in Colorado. Florida's humidity was never her friend so the change in seasons appeals to her. While involved in LBGTQ rights and liberal political causes she is working toward IT certification to further her in her career. Her cats, Tegan and Ashe, give her the paws-on love we cannot since we live so far from each other.

I continue to have a relationship with Marlene. She sends me cards for every occasion, and letters which often include her latest drawings of cats or women pastors. My phone inevitably rings on special days, showing her on the caller ID, and we chat easily. I sought her permission to include our story in this book and she happily agreed.

Would my life have been better if I had not chosen the Road Less Traveled? Being contentedly retired and thus having the leisure to assess that question, I will say that I have noticed a gradual interior movement toward an acceptance of all that has been. I still like asking God questions and looking for answers, which has led me to this conclusion. Pretend Margie, the Elephant in the room, that darn Cinder Block Room, Mr. D, Parky, my bucket, and My Victim Story will all be part of me forever. God did not cause them, but used them to form me. However, they are largely part of my past, not my future. I suppose that is my latest Holy Ground.

ENDNOTES

1. Kevin Leman, *The Birth Order Book: Why You Are the Way You Are* (Grand Rapids, MI, Revell, 2009).

2. Ibid., 155.

3. Rob Bell, *Velvet Elvis: Repainting the Christian Faith* (Grand Rapids, MI, Zondervan, 2005), 24.

4. Ibid.

5. Ibid., 25.

ACKNOWLEDGMENTS

I began writing what became this book in order to "get stuff out" and to try to heal myself. It has been over six years since I completed the first draft. I hold Penelope Love from Citrine Publishing in high regard. To have found her has been the blessing that I needed to move past my anxieties regarding publishing as a neophyte author. She guided me through a new-to-me process with enthusiasm and genuine admiration for this work.

Collaborating with Jaime Cox as she edited my manuscript was a joyful experience. She kept me focused on improving and streamlining where needed, as well as giving me the "attagirls" that helped me understand that my story has the power to help others.

I am grateful to many loving souls who championed my writing in some way. Thanks to my writing instructor, Julie Gilbert, who moved me from novice to more seasoned in my writing. Lisa Geovjian and Fran Gragg read early drafts and gave me valuable input. The people in my writers' groups, Pat, Cheryl, Karen, Dawn, Susan, Lisa, and Jim, helped me learn how to "show and not tell." Seminary friend, Paula Gravelle Turner, was an early enthusiast of my writing.

I thank the many people in the parishes in which I served as pastor. The supporters rallied around my vision for ministry and jumped into the future with me. It was always a joy and privilege to look out on their faces when I preached, and to see the smiles, nodding heads, and sometimes even tears. That always showed me God-is-love in real time. To those I disappointed or angered, I continue to pray that God can heal any wounds I may have caused and that forgiveness can eventually bring a glow of light in their memories of me. Being a leader in congregations of expectant and faith-filled people led me to ponder profound things about God and the universe, examine myself, and continually work to become a more spiritually-grounded pastor and theologian.

Finally, family. Over a span of thirty-five years, my husband attended scores of worship services to listen to my sermons and to be my strong helpmate, even though God remains elusive to him. His quiet presence in the sanctuary buoyed me. His willingness to be the hands-on evening parent when I was at yet another meeting made mothering young girls much more manageable for me. He intuitively knew to stay out of all congregational drama so that his voice would never have been mistaken for mine. Instead, he built walls, literally (not cinder block, but Sheetrock), more than once in church buildings, taught teenagers (who loved him) in Sunday School, and came to my rescue more times than I can say when something went wrong or needed attention in a church building, like faulty air conditioning, furniture that needed rearranging, or a pesky computer problem. Most of all he has loved me, something I have never doubted even when Mr. D tried to mask that.

Beyond any lasting imprints I may have left behind in the congregations I have led is the legacy of my children. Lynn and Angela have been my life's best work. I happily enjoyed sewing many outfits for them. Each time they wore one of them I could proudly admire my creativity. As the alpha parent, I was cheerleader, teacher, listener, and nag and they know I have not always been soft and squishy. My hope is that the sewing of life skills I tried to impart have contributed to their being

fine peopl...

sing to others.

created from

endless.

vesting your

ivite you to

storweiss54

m.

PUBLISHER'S NOTE

Thank you for reading Marjorie Weiss's *Praying on Empty: A Female Pastor's Story*. If you enjoyed this book, you can support the author by helping others find it. Here are some suggestions for your consideration:

- Write an online customer review wherever books are sold
- Gift this book to family and friends
- Share a photo of the book on social media and tag #pastormarjorieweiss and #prayingonempty
- Bring in Pastor Marjorie Weiss as a speaker for your club or organization
- Suggest *Praying on Empty* to your local book club
- For bulk order inquiries, contact Citrine Publishing at (828) 585-7030 or publisher@citrinepublishing.com
- Connect with Pastor Marjorie Weiss at www.facebook.com/pastorweiss54 www.prayingonempty.com

Made in the USA
Columbia, SC
19 June 2023